THE TENACIOUS PURSUIT

OF PEACE

THE TENACIOUS PURSUIT OF

PEACE

WHERE TO GO WHEN SUCCESS IS NOT ENOUGH

BY MADELEINE MACRAE

THE TENACIOUS PURSUIT
OF PEACE

WHERE TO GO WHEN SUCCESS IS NOT ENOUGH

First Printing, October 2023

ISBN: 979-8-8727060-7-6

Published in the United States by Weeva, Inc.
Cover and design by Kaitlyn Tostado of Weeva, Inc.

Weeva, Inc.
Austin, TX
https://bookstore.weeva.com
Hello@weeva.com

MadeleineMacrae.com
Hello@MadeleineMacrae.com

In loving memory of an unshakable believer, amazing storyteller,
best bad-joke-teller, and, most importantly to me,
my constant support and my Dad, Howard MacRae.
Love and miss you always. Rest in peace. See you in Heaven!

ACKNOWLEDGMENTS

THERE ARE SO MANY PEOPLE TO THANK, names to name, experiences to acknowledge, that it's hard to know exactly where to start, so let me start at the beginning.

I want to make a special word of thanks to my Mom. Mom, I owe much of the woman I am today to you. You've always been there for me. Supporting me, encouraging me, praying for me, cheering me on even when you don't really know why I'm doing what I'm doing or why anyone would do the things I do. You've made many sacrifices to give me the life, the family, the faith and the education that I was lucky to have, and I hope you know that you mean the world to me. I'll always be grateful for your loving support and your steady presence in my life.

Being the high verbal processor that I am, there is no way the stories in this book would have been able to come pouring out on the page unless they had first been shared with others. So to everyone who has heard me tell these stories, more times than they probably wanted to hear them, most especially to my sister and dearest friend, Missy, and to my endlessly patient brother, Mike, thank you. Thank you for all of the early morning and late-night calls and for all the countless ways you are there for me in good moments and in rough ones. I love you and wouldn't want to do life without you.

To my sweet son, Noah. Becoming your Mom changed me forever. I never knew that my heart could hold so much love. You have made me grow in ways I could never have expected. You have my heart. I'm endlessly proud of you.

To my bonus son, Jacob, I'm so proud of the man you're becoming. Having the privilege of being your bonus mom has shaped me and meant more to me than you know.

To the man who made me a Mom in the first place, Paul Hannan, rest in peace my friend. And to the man whose baby I was, my Dad, Howard MacRae, I love and miss you endlessly. May the angels reward all of the wonderful things you did and still do for me.

A very special thanks goes out to my coaches and mentors along the way, many of whom I'm privileged to call friends including Michael Lee, Jean-Philippe Demaël, Michele Gunderson, Andrea J. Lee, Elsbeth Meuth and Freddy Zental Weaver, Eleanor Beaton, Sherris Cottier-Shank, and Sam Horn. As well as to the many therapists who have helped me along the path of healing and to the incredible individuals I've had the honor to coach and mentor whether in my corporate life or throughout the many iterations of my entrepreneurial adventures. You have helped make the woman I am today and I'm forever grateful.

This book wouldn't ever be the incredible compilation of stories it has become without the guidance and support of my bold and oh-so-helpful book coach, Kim Galloway, without the nudge of my business partner and co-founder at Legacy Leadership Institute, Thomas MacDonald, or without the professional touches of my editor Kate Bonnycastle, my logo designer Rebecca Bratz, my publisher Kimberly Gorsuch and her incredible team at Weeva, especially Kaitlyn and Lolo. Much love and appreciation to each of you!

And, to every person whose intersection with my life has enriched it with the experiences and the insights, the joys and the sorrows, the healing and the growth that shows up in the stories that grace these pages or even in those that didn't show up in this book. Each and every one of you hold a very dear place in my heart and I'm profoundly and forever grateful.

CONTENTS

PREFACE 13

CHAPTER ONE: THE WHOLE TRUTH 19
    PRACTICE: START WITH CLARITY 36

CHAPTER TWO: KNOW WHO YOU ARE 39
    PRACTICE: EXPLORING WHO YOU ARE 56

CHAPTER THREE: KNOW WHERE YOU ARE 59
    PRACTICE: HONORING YOUR GPS 82

CHAPTER FOUR: NARRATIVE CONTROL 85
    PRACTICE: CREATING YOUR NARRATIVE 106

CHAPTER FIVE: THE NUDGE 109
    THE SKIN 124

CHAPTER SIX: LIGHTNING ROD MOMENTS 127
    PRACTICE: THE MIRROR EXERCISE 144

CHAPTER SEVEN: RADICLE GRATITUDE 147
    PRACTICE: 21 DAY CHALLENGE 164

CHAPTER EIGHT: LETTING GO 167
    PRACTICE: THE INVENTORY OF LETTING GO 188

CHAPTER NINE: START YOUR OWN TABLE 191
    PRACTICE: WHAT'S YOUR LUCK SCORE? 208

CHAPTER TEN: TRUE NORTH 211

EPILOGUE 233
    LUCEAT PRAYER BEFORE WRITING 241
ABOUT THE AUTHOR 245

PREFACE

**STORY HAS BEEN DANCING IN MY CONSCIOUSNESS
FROM AS EARLY AS I COULD WRITE.**

A T SIX YEARS OLD, I was working on what I was convinced was the riveting tale of "The Cat and the Mouse." I would sit at the wooden desk in our basement, carefully crafting each sentence, forming each letter of each word on the off-white, ultra-wide-ruled, extra-long paper. Each time I finished the last sentence on a page, I would rush up the stairs to read my work to my Mom. She would encourage me to read just the new page, but every time I would tell her that she wouldn't enjoy the story—the whole drama—unless she heard it from the top. I always insisted on it. And she would patiently listen as I reread words already so familiar to her from the prior dozen trips up the stairs. She would let me read what I had written and she would encourage me to continue. And she's done just the same for this book.

That childhood first manuscript sits in a folder in my writing desk, and, though it will never become pages of a printed book, it engraved upon my heart the love of storytelling, of writing, and of language that has followed me through my life.

In junior high I learned how to write a well-crafted essay, in high school I delved more deeply into language and poetry, and by the time I made it to college I was in love with literature and made it my major.

Story has been ever-present in my life and it's no accident that the very first personal development retreat I ever went to was called Story Freedom.

If you're reading this book, it's because you are curious about personal development. Maybe you feel the slightest knocking at the door of your heart or maybe a loud, insistent beating, and you're searching for an answer.

I too have searched.

I searched in many ways over many years and it wasn't until after the death of my Dad—my ever-supportive cheerleader and confidante—that I really began to consider that it might be time to take the work, the deep inner work that I do with my private coaching clients, and share it more broadly.

You see, when I started my coaching and consulting firm back in 2015, my mission was to make the secrets of the most successful not secrets any more. And I started where I felt most competent, on the tactics of business—the hard skills that it was easy for me to teach: sales, marketing, process. And as I learned how to teach those skills, I began to realize that mastering the tactics, the practical how-to, wasn't enough to be truly excellent.

All the tactics in the world won't make you successful if you don't know how to work with the people.

How to get people to do the things that you need them to do, how to communicate, what to communicate, when to communicate it, how to encourage, how to correct, how to inspire. So I quickly started to teach more of those management and leadership skills. I led leadership intensives and started to work with companies large and small to develop their leaders and their teams.

The more leaders I coached, the more I saw that the very best managers and leaders don't start on the outside, they start from within. They know themselves, they understand themselves and they support their teams in working within the frameworks that will allow them all to shine, to succeed, to win.

As I was watching this truth play out in my professional work, I was also on a multi-year journey of intense healing and deep inner work. I was feeling more capable and confident in giving what I had found for myself, so I started to weave that into my private work. I began to help my clients understand themselves more fully, to be intentional about not only their business strategy, but about getting where they wanted to be in life as well as in their businesses.

And it was after the death of my Dad in 2020 that I decided to be a little more bold about doing this personal development work. I led my very first virtual retreat in January 2021 and continued to help my clients—who were looking for business success—to look inward, journey inward, and be the leaders and the men and women they truly wanted to become.

But I wasn't quite ready to let go of the tactics of business. I had such an incredible repertoire of work, of best practices and practical advice, of sales training and management resources, of checklists and templates and handbooks. I had hundreds of things I had created and that were being used in some of the best businesses of my industry and I couldn't, in good conscience, leave it all languishing on the shelf, available only to the few who would invest in private coaching with me.

So I didn't leave it languishing.

I built it out even more. I turned it into Homepro Toolbox—a digital resource center with hundreds of short videos and templates and done-for-you business content—and launched it as a whole new company. And it was only when that crowning jewel of my practical business coaching was complete that I was able to turn my focus right here, to this work. To this book.

It took building out another business for me to be able to be ready to play full out. To share with you the real, raw, unfiltered truth of my journey beyond the glittering wall of success. To show you, in story, what it means to journey inwards, to seek something and maybe, just maybe, to find it.

And I play full out.

I don't leave anything off-limits. Not the sweet stuff, not the tough stuff.

I go there.

I tell the hard stories.

It might be that you find yourself stopping in the midst of the painful parts of my story.

Continue to read even when you feel like stopping. I promise I never leave you—at least in my stories—in unresolved pain. The painful parts are not the end of the story. The healing can begin when the pain stops. Sometimes just surviving day to day is the best we can do; but take courage, continue to walk, seek the help you need, know that there is immense strength right here, right now, even at your lowest, it is there. And beyond the pain there is joy, there is light, there is peace.

If you're feeling deeply triggered, know that is your inner wisdom telling you that you have unresolved trauma. Those triggers happen when something is mirroring where *you are* in your journey right now or where something is unresolved that wants to seek resolution, healing. If that happens, seek the support and the guidance of an expert, a professional, a therapist.

Beyond the pain there is joy, there is light, there is peace. It may take some work to get there, but I'm telling you it is so worth it!

Don't get stuck in the painful parts of the stories.

Move through the pain to the promise.

Know that a regular girl who grew up in a blue-collar neighborhood outside of Detroit, Michigan, made it through trauma and the painful parts of her story and is here, writing these words to you, so that you know that you can too.

This is possible for you!

And I didn't get here in spite of anything that has happened. I got here, in a place of peace, because of everything that happened.

If you're like me and are looking for a place to start, come along with me in this book of story and of invitation. Journey, with me, inward to go upwards.

It's a wild and fantastic ride!

CHAPTER 1

THE WHOLE TRUTH

"An act of faith often exacts a leap in the dark."

— FATHER GABRIEL OF ST. MARY MAGDALEN

MY HANDS.

MY HANDS WERE SHAKING UNCONTROLLABLY.

RESTING THERE ON THE LECTERN, halfway up the stack of white copier paper with double-spaced lines of text, their trembling was getting so bad that it was jiggling the sheets and making it hard for my eyes to keep track of the words.

I had to do something.

Watching my hands shake was distracting me terribly and making me feel incredibly nervous. More nervous than I already was—which was already a lot.

I slid them down the slanted wooden face of the stand, out of my direct line of sight. As my palms skimmed the surface, I could feel the satiny finish of the handcrafted wood. My fingers alighted on the bottom lip of the lectern and I rested them there. The smooth texture making contact with the pads of my fingertips soothed my nerves.

Whether my hands were still trembling or not I didn't know, but at least I could no longer see the visual reminder of my nervous energy.

I hadn't stopped speaking once throughout this whole swirling dervish of emotional turmoil, and when those darn shaking hands weren't in my line of sight anymore, I took a breath and turned my full attention back to the words I was reading.

I had read those words dozens and dozens of times—sometimes aloud, other times to myself. I knew them incredibly well. I loved the quotes. I savored the message. It was exactly what I wanted to say. I had poured hours of effort into crafting each sentence and wanted it to be perfect, so I had practiced reading it over and over. But today, today was different. Today, I was reading those precious words in front of the whole student body and all of our school community. My classmates and fellow schoolgirls, our families, the teachers, parents, benefactors of the school—the whole community was there.

It was a good speech, full of the idealistic vigor of youth, brimming over with the joy of pursuing a new chapter of life. And it was equally wistful about the life and friends I was leaving behind.

Standing there in my white cap and gown with my gold and black tassel dangling on the side of my face, I would never have imagined that decades later, I would be a professional speaker who could grab the mic in front of a room of hundreds without feeling a moment of hesitation, doubt, or stage fright.

That day I was certainly nervous.

It was graduation day.

And I was giving my valedictorian speech.

Within the first few minutes of standing at the lectern, I remember looking feverishly for my parents in the crowd.

My eyes were mostly glued to the paper in front of me and I was reading the words verbatim. I didn't know any other way to give a speech. I couldn't look up for long because I hadn't memorized the whole thing and ad libbing wasn't even a glimmer of a thought. But I wanted to find them in the sea of faces.

I kept looking up and glancing around.

I knew my Mom and Dad were there—they had flown in from Michigan for the occasion—but I didn't know where they were sitting and I couldn't find them in my short, searching glances. After I had looked quite a few times, I could feel a little sadness and disappointment creeping over me. I was standing there speaking because of my parents. I had worked hard day after day, week after week, year after year—not for the prestige of being valedictorian, but to show my parents that their considerable sacrifices in sending me to boarding school were not in vain.

I wanted to be excellent to show them my gratitude.

My diligent studies had not only done that, but they had also landed me at the top of my class. I hadn't ever considered I would be valedictorian—in fact, we had called another girl in my class Val for years because we thought she was the heir apparent. I must admit that I felt a little sheepish when I found out that I was claiming that honor. It felt like I had accidentally taken it from her. I hadn't been striving to do it, but there I was. She and I hadn't ever discussed it, but I'm sure she was as disappointed as I was surprised.

She had been our salutatorian and her speech had been great.

As I was starting to feel the deep disappointment of not finding my parents, I spotted my favorite teacher of all time, Mother Mary Bernard. She was the only nun I had ever called "Dad" accidentally. She had been my very first homeroom teacher years ago and she had this warmth about her that made me feel close to her like my family. I could see her gentle soul through those kind, brown eyes and the reassuring and proud look she gave me helped me settle my mind, soothe my heart and proceed forward.

Through her, I somehow knew my parents saw me too. And felt how she felt—maybe even more. I still felt nervous. But I started to feel happy, excited, and proud. Very, very proud.

It was one of the first big moments in my life where pride felt like exactly the correct response.

You see, for the first couple of decades of my life I had a very rigid and disempowering understanding of pride and of humility. Humility was presented as a sense of lowliness, taking the last seat, not seeking the spotlight, and it was proffered as the core indicator of holiness. Pride was its antithesis—glory-mongering, leaping to the front of the line, putting yourself, your ideas, your wants before those of others.

And I was also raised with the firm belief that those to whom much is given, much is expected. Our gifts are not for ourselves alone—they are to be used, increased and shared, and, even as a very young child, I was excited to do that. I somehow sensed that I had been given many gifts and talents and I wanted to use them full out.

But when I used my talents, it would catapult me to the top spot, the front of the line, the spotlight. When I would speak, people would listen. When I would offer ideas, they would be the ones that would be done.

It felt good and right, but the only word I had to describe that was bossy. And it wasn't an endearing term. So, I struggled to make sense of what I intuitively knew about myself without an empowering framework to support that insight and the tools to use my gifts without bulldozing other people. When my lack of skill or my hard-charging nature, unmitigated by finesse, would end up with me being too forceful my mom would parry back with, "Honey, pride cometh before the fall."

I did not want to be proud.

I wanted to be good.

So, I felt that I had to tamp down my hard-driving nature, to curb the bend of my bossiness, to hold back my ideas and suggestions so that others would have a chance to shine.

And it was a heavy burden for my little shoulders to carry.

I felt like I was between a rock and a hard place. I was expected to be humble, lowly, not puffed up. I was supposed to go to the lowest seat and never seek to be exalted. And yet, I was expected to use my gifts to their fullest extent and those gifts were the very things that made me the center of attention, put me at the front of the line, earned me the spot at the head of my class.

The words that I heard in the Bible, Matthew 5:16, "So let your light shine before men, that they may see your good works and give glory to your Father who is in heaven," felt to me like the most inspiring rallying cry and an intense slap in the face all at once.

I did not know how to shine and not shine at the same time.

It was a problem for me.

Emotionally, spiritually, intellectually, I was in a conundrum.

During my years in boarding school, the focus on intellectual development, the intensity of our coursework, and the rigid structure of our daily schedule left very little room for me to feel uncomfortable with my gifts. In fact, I wasn't thinking about my gifts and strengths at all during that phase of my life. I was so focused on excellence in all of my classes and on doing all of the work we were assigned, following all of the rules, keeping to our predictable schedule, that whether I was good at something or not wasn't part of the paradigm.

But I was still very aware of my need to be humble, and I had translated that into minimizing and side-stepping compliments, avoiding being publicly recognized, hiding—sometimes in plain sight.

Yet here I was, on graduation day, standing in full view of everyone, sharing my thoughts and my words of hope and inspiration. Being seen, being visible, being commended, earning the top seat in our tiny little class.

The remainder of the ceremony and everything that transpired between walking off the stage and settling into a standing spot at the top of the gravel path outside of the auditorium are all a blur of excitement and a swirl of faces, dresses, suits.

The first person I remember hugging me and telling me I had done a great job was one of my closest friends. She didn't need to say much to transmit the warmth of her happiness. Her hug and the sincerity of her words landed right in the part of my heart that was still a bit nervous and wobbly and helped to melt away the shakiness. It made my insides feel as strong and sure-footed as my outsides did.

She knew how hard I had worked to get to where I was and how much I had poured into the speech itself. She was as happy for me as I was for myself and a wave of relief washed over me when she hugged me, leaving me feeling calm and steady.

The jitters were gone, the doubt evaporated. Only the joy and pride remained.

Her congratulatory hug seemed to break an invisible thread that had been holding back a sea of people and suddenly a mad rush of happy, excited people started to pour over to me. Person after person came up to me. My parents and family finally found their way to me. Teachers, students from the younger grades, parents of friends. Some of them were dear friends and boarder-buddies, others were total random strangers I didn't know.

They all unleashed on me what felt like an endless stream of congratulatory words, hugs, handshakes. The first person had hardly even stopped talking before the second started. I was pelted from all sides with "Great job!" "Awesome speech." "Well done!" "Congrats!" "Great speech." "Wow! That was great."

My whole self wanted to defer and side-step their praise. I wanted to say things like "Oh! No big deal." "Gosh! Thanks but I'm sure it could have been way better." "Oh, you know! I love to write, so it was really nothing."

I wanted to dodge the compliments like I usually did, but I couldn't.

There were so many people and things were moving so fast and praise was pouring in from all sides. I simply didn't have the time to say much at all, much less the mental bandwidth to think of a kind way to duck their sincere words of praise without being rude, so I had to settle for "Thank you!" over and over and over again.

Not because I wanted to accept their compliments graciously — I didn't. With every fiber of my being, I wanted to hide out from their praise or at least minimize the compliments somehow. It felt uncomfortable to be congratulated, to be seen and recognized like this, to have people put me under such a bright spotlight.

But I had no choice but to smile and be gracious.

All day long, for the rest of the day, and even for the rest of the weekend, I got a master course in accepting a compliment with a smile and a genuine word of thanks.

A permanent rewiring was happening in my brain in real time.

While I didn't know it then, that day was the beginning of the breakage of something that had held me tightly and uncomfortably.

It was my first visceral experience of acceptance.

I was letting the truth of what they said stand, without minimization, explanation, or denial.

The flow of congratulatory words on graduation day planted a seed of change in my experience of what it felt like and my understanding of what true humility really is.

The irony is that just as I experienced a real moment of genuine acceptance from the outside, the inward movement of my humility journey shifted back to the more difficult narrative of my much younger years.

As I left the structured environment of boarding school and started to create my own way in the world, I began to resent my gifts more and more.

Many things were warring within me. I wanted to be like other people. I wanted to be living congruently with my conscience and to use my gifts for great good. And I wanted to be humble too. And each one of those things required something so different of me, or so I thought, that it felt like I was living in an immovable, internal gridlock.

As the years progressed, I got through college and many of my close friends started partnering up, getting married, and having kids. I felt more and more different and alone.

I wanted to go with the flow of what everyone else seemed to do and to want.

I was tired of trying to reconcile my humility-and-pride conflict. I was tired of carrying the burden of being multi-talented.

I just wanted to be normal.

I remember one moment when I was particularly upset over feeling so different, so other, so alone.

I was driving back home after some painfully awkward situation had just happened and I was talking to God. Actually, I was yelling at God, giving Him a very strong piece of my mind. I was in my car, by myself, driving under an overpass, about to get on the freeway and I was shouting at the top of my lungs.

I was ranting.

Tears were streaming down my face and the only thing keeping my hands from shaking was the death grip I had on the steering wheel. I was demanding that God take away my gifts.

"I didn't ask for all of this.

I don't want it. All of these things are just too much for me.

Take it away.

Take them all away.

I just want to be like everyone else."

I was begging to be released from my innermost desires to do more, be more. I didn't want to hunger for knowledge anymore. I didn't want to yearn for excellence. I was tired of wanting to reach high and go far.

I just wanted to be like everyone else.

I wanted to want the white picket fence, and the husband, and the 1.5 kids that everyone else wanted. I wanted to feel content with a simple life without big ambitions, without the yearning in my heart to shine and to lead.

I wanted to be left alone.

To have these desires leave me alone.

I was crying out, with my voice, from the depths of my soul, to be anyone other than who I was.

Throughout my life, I've had several of those moments of big rants to the skies, beseeching God for mercy, sitting in my car, laying out my pain, and begging for a path away from it. And while the answer is rarely immediate, it is always given.

When we can accept where we are—even if it is a moment of seeking deliverance from that very place—and when we can ask for what we need, our clarity and our humility pierces the veil of the unseen and carries our words to the heart of the Almighty who then conspires to support us.

He gives us what we need.

For me, it showed up as an incredibly important lightbulb moment that I had within a month or so of my raging outcry in my car. When it happened, I didn't perceive it as a response to my plea, but in hindsight, the response is so crystal clear. The insight I was given radically shifted my perspective and broke free that seemingly impenetrable gridlock, the very gridlock that was making me want relief and deliverance from it.

And it had everything to do with humility.

I don't know what I was doing or reading when I stumbled upon it, and I am sure that, amid the decades of Catholic elementary school, high school, and college, I had heard this definition before, but at this stage of my life I finally heard it afresh. I understood its implications and allowed it to take root in my heart and to change my life.

It was the definition of humility.

The definition was from the Principles of the First Order of the Society of Saint Francis and said, "Humility is the recognition of the truth about God and ourselves."

The recognition of the truth.

Stunning reality.

Humility was not about being abject or lowly or putting our big, beautiful, bright, shining lights in a secret hiding place and pretending they didn't exist. It wasn't about hiding or trying to squash our gifts so they wouldn't be so bright after all, so intimidating to others.

It wasn't about making myself more relatable. It wasn't about making my gifts more palatable.

It was about knowing my gifts. Recognizing how great they are to me but how small they are in the greater cosmos.

It was about understanding my gifts, deepening them and using them full-out, without the smallest shadow of embarrassment or apology.

This wonderful moment of profound enlightenment coincided with a shift that happened for me in 2006 when I read *Now, Discover*

Your Strengths by Donald O. Clifton and Marcus Buckingham. Between the new-found sense of discovering my strengths, the encouragement to explore them and the call to radical acceptance of them, I started a slow, multi-decade process of transformation from the inside out.

Being humble, you see, isn't about pretending to be something you're not.

It is not about faking it.

It's about owning the truth about yourself and being neither depressed nor inflated by it.

The gifts and talents that we have are not within our control.

You are who you are. All of it.

Your stories and traumas, your triumphs and your joys, your lightning rod moments and the way you ignore or embrace them. All of it is yours.

One evening in midsummer 2018, I was having dinner with two of my close friends. We gathered at the home of the most artistic of our triumvirate—a beautiful and accomplished woman whose work as a gem carver had reached as far and high as to be featured at the Smithsonian and whose work as a hypnotherapist continues to sound the depths of the human soul. We had already had wine and cheese while we filled each other in on the happenings of the prior month in our lives and businesses and were progressing onto dinner.

We were a merry little party, laughing off the trials and disappointments, sharing the successes, doing our best to help each other stay grounded and optimistic as we figured out the pathway forward in our lives and in our businesses.

When you're building a business, it can sometimes look like an elegant ascent up a noble staircase. The walls of the staircase are high and, from the outside, you see the head dip and return, disappearing out of sight every few seconds and then re-emerging further up the flight of stairs. As you observe this, you imagine that the business owner is gracefully climbing the staircase, unencumbered, effortlessly. But what you don't see behind the high wall is that everytime the head vanishes, it's not because of the angle of the stairs or a prolonged landing, but because the individual has stumbled—sometimes flat out face-planted—and then has found their footing again and managed to make it to the next stair, upright and unharmed.

This collection of women understood that journey because they were walking it alongside me. We were all building something and we told each other about our stumbles and the wisdom we gained from them as well as our successes and how we arrived at those too. It was a collaborative, introspective, supportive, understanding group and I looked forward to our casual monthly gatherings.

On this particular evening we were talking about that strange and perilous entrepreneurial ascent and I was sharing how good it felt to be with women who understood what it was like. I was telling them how I had, throughout the course of my life, so often found myself in rooms where I had felt uninspired and uninspiring. It had happened in conference ballrooms crowded with people, in small groups of acquaintances, and even in one-on-one conversations.

"I would find myself sitting there," I told them, "mute and uncomfortable, with nothing to say, feeling like I had nothing of value to contribute."

Boring.

Awkward.

Out of place.

It's one of the loneliest feelings in the world.

I know that I take a little while to warm up and I've always attributed that to the fact that I'm more of a response-driven communicator than a spark. I wait to see where people are and what they are discussing rather than charging forward and driving the conversation. And I do hate small talk. I never really seem to know what to say. But get me talking about big ideas and making deep connections and I have plenty to share, plenty to say.

It's always baffled me that I'm friendly, open, optimistic and predominantly extroverted but can still be so incredibly socially awkward like that.

I explained all this to my friends. "It's been happening since I was a kid. I felt it differently when I was little, but it's always been there. I just felt a bit odd—not in the loner way or in the brainiac who can do complex math in their minds way. I had friends and was socially well-adjusted but I just knew that I didn't seem to tick like other people."

They listened as I talked and gave me empathetic encouragement with nods of their heads, knowing raises of their eyebrows or the corners of their mouths, or little supportive sounds like hmm and yeah. They were actively listening and encouraging me to continue my monologue.

I looked from one kind face to the other as I searched for the right way to describe what I had felt.

"I've looked for stories that captured how I felt. There was *The Ugly Duckling*, but I didn't feel that applied very well because I didn't go from feeling ugly to feeling and being beautiful. I've always looked about the same. But there was something about me that resonated with that story."

Maybe it pointed to the fact that I was in the wrong flock of birds.

"I haven't found the words to describe it," I told my support group, "or the right analogy yet. I've always wanted to say that I felt like an eagle among chickens but that doesn't feel very honoring to the amazing people I grew up with. Calling them chickens feels disrespectful and rude. And makes it seem like I feel that I am better than they are. And that couldn't be further from the truth. That's not how I feel at all. I love them. I care for them. I appreciate them and see so many admirable and beautiful traits in them.

"We are just different.

"We want different things.

"I want to fly high and spread my wings and soar.

"They want to stay with their feet firmly planted on the ground.

"I want my space and my freedom. They want to cozy up together and huddle really closely.

"What's an animal like that called? What's something that everyone loves?"

We sat looking at each other in silence. I was processing something that had been in my heart for a long time and the answer hung in the air.

Nobody interrupted the silence.

"A penguin!" I suddenly shouted.

"That's it!" they all chimed in.

"Absolutely. That's how I've felt. An eagle amid penguins. And everyone loves penguins. They are incredible birds. How many movies and documentaries are there about penguins?"

We all beamed. Sherris, our host, confirmed in a musing kind of voice, "Yes. That feels right. Penguins. An eagle amid penguins."

The room suddenly went from riveted concentration on my words as I verbally hashed out this long-germinating idea to a buzz of chatter.

The ladies loved the idea that had come from my stream-of-consciousness share with them. They talked about how that analogy seemed to strike the right balance between respect and difference. How it was more about being than looking, how it spoke to the differences of needs and nature rather than aesthetics.

Cheryl, the recently retired engineer of our group who was building a business that would go on to incredible heights and who had also raised her son on her own said to me, "If you felt this way, it's likely that Noah will too. You should turn this into a story for him."

It was a fantastic idea and I immediately said that I would.

I began writing that very week.

About a month or two later Noah started school. It was then that his own differences started to become undeniably clear. His unusualness was even more apparent than mine and it unfolded over the course of the next several years. We came to know his differences, to be able to identify and label them, and to learn how to navigate through. That was all happening while I was writing the story and it fused itself in the narrative.

What began as a story about myself to help my son, whose apple couldn't have fallen too far from my tree, started to become an amalgamation of my experiences and his. And the little story that I started at that warm kitchen table in the fading daylight of a summer evening took on an existence of its own. It slowly went from a super short story to a long poem to a manuscript for a book. From there it was fully illustrated as a children's story and went on to get published and to reach Amazon best-seller status in our primary category.

It was a wildly unexpected journey for both of us and on Christmas morning, 2022, Noah held the very first copy of *The Unusual Penguin* in his hands.

My favorite lines of the book are spread over the final few pages:

"Penguins and eagles are incredible creatures.
But if judged as the same, they fall short on features.
Neither can do what the other one can.
One bird loves the sky, the other the land.

An eagle, you see, isn't unusual at all
But if you think he's a penguin he'll certainly feel small.

So if you feel small, unusual or strange,
Don't jump to the conclusion that you have to change.
You are perfectly perfect just as you are.
Find your own wings, you'll fly high and go far."

Your strengths and your weaknesses, you see, are consistent parts of yourself—parts that you can grow or parts that you can diminish. Parts that you can allow to be vulnerabilities and to make you feel strange, different, other, exposed; or parts that can be a source of incredible strength and power.

It is a *choice.*

It is *your* choice.

It is *always* your choice.

You get to embrace the truth—the whole truth, the full truth—of all that you truly are.

START WITH CLARITY

♥

Sometimes I struggle with road rage. Not the get-out-of-the-car-and-yell-at-someone type, more the imagine-that-I-could-ram-the-car-in-front-of-me-without-consequences type.

Over the years I've learned that when I feel triggered behind the wheel, when I'm rushing and anxious, when I'm unable to tolerate the slightly self-centered carelessness of others, it really has nothing to do with the other driver or even with driving at all.

It has to do with me.

What's happening in my life.

With deep needs that are going unmet.

When I can't handle being cut off, I've found it's often because somewhere else in my life I am feeling not heard, not seen, not understood. I'm crowded and feel like I, as a person, lack space to inhabit freely. When I'm sparked to undue anger by other people being what I feel is rude on the road, I've learned to look within. To ask myself what I need.

Most of us carry deep wounds around not being seen, not being heard, or not feeling good enough.

But those wounds don't have to be a life sentence.

As an adult, we can give to ourselves the things that we need and we don't need to externalize or to seek it from others. But the very first step is getting clear.

Sometimes we are unwilling to look at our own woundedness, to ask ourselves if we are at peace with where we are in the macro of our lives, to ponder if we truly know and love ourselves just as we are, wrinkles and bumps and size and shape and all.

But when you have the courage to look within and uncover that woundedness and decide to give yourself what you need at an emotional, psychological level, you can change your future.

And step one is being willing to look. Examined under a brighter light, those scary monsters are less scary than they are when they stay lurking in the hidden, dark recesses of our minds.

Don't be afraid to bring them out into the light.

Don't be afraid to get clear.

Take things deeper at:
www.madeleinemacrae.com/gifts

♡ Madeleine

CHAPTER 2

KNOW WHO YOU ARE

"The splendor of the rose and the lily's whiteness do not
deprive the violet of its scent nor make less ravishing the
daisy's charm... If every little flower wished to be a rose,
Nature would lose her spring adornments, and the field
would be no longer enameled with their varied flowers."

— THERESE OF LISIEUX

IT WAS WEIRDLY AWKWARD.

I WAS MAKING THE LOOPING ASCENT up each of the spiraling
levels, getting closer and closer to my designated parking spot.
The walls were thick, gray concrete and the light from outside was
finding its way through the perforated walls but it was by no means
as bright and sunny inside as it was in the sunshine outside.

I had to squeeze past huge concrete pillars and make my way
around narrow turns. It was a drive I had made often, but one that
I never enjoyed. My muscle memory, more than my skill, was in
charge of managing the process without scraping the sides of my
car against the walls or other descending cars.

The busy, bustling traffic from the visitors and day-parkers that
filled the temporary spots on the lower floors had subsided and I was
navigating through the resident parking area undisturbed.

I was on the phone with a man I had recently started dating. He lived in Miami, and we were just beginning to explore the possibility of a long-distance relationship. We initially met through business many years prior and were only a few days into exploring something beyond a casual sort of professional connection. While he didn't know me extraordinarily well, the many years of our acquaintance-ship meant that he knew me more than most.

The ambiance of the late afternoon had felt alive and peaceful.

But I had just said something that made my own eyebrows rise and my eyes go wide.

I can't remember our exact conversation, but I remember it was pleasant and light. I was telling him a story or filling him in on my day, or maybe we were discussing some upcoming travel plans. While the specifics of the conversation are vague, the moment isn't. I was talking and was wrapping up what I was saying when I suddenly used a big, multisyllabic word at the end of my phrase. I don't have any idea which of my crazy vocabulary words it may have been, but I know it was an uncommon word and a big long one at that.

The second the word left my mouth, I paused. He paused too.

The tension was palpable.

I continued to drive up to my parking space which was now very close.

The conversation seemed to be suspended in midair even as I continued to drive.

I felt very uncomfortable and, as I pulled into my space and put my car in park, I started to hyperfocus on the fabric of the passenger seat in my now parked car. It was dark charcoal black, woven with a tight weave, interspersed with a few dark gray fibers.

I was preoccupying my mind, trying to distract myself from my own discomfort.

The only thing I could think to say was, "Sorry about that." And it blurted out before I had a chance to stop it.

"Sorry? Why are you sorry?"

"Oh! I just never use words like that," I replied, trying to sound easy-breezy and casual, knowing full well that I was anything but that at the moment.

It was clear that he was a bit confused by my awkward pause, my apology and then my blow-off statement. I could feel it, but I didn't really know how to make it better.

"Words like what?" he pressed.

"You know, big, long, complicated words. I just don't really use them." My voice sounded both apologetic and guilty as I said that. I was acting like I had done something truly offensive. I was behaving as though I had transgressed some big, important boundary with my vocabulary choice—because, in fact, I had.

I had just broken one of my own internal rules of behavior. It was a rule that he didn't know anything about and that I hadn't articulated to myself or to anyone else, for that matter, but it was a big one for me.

I felt the overwhelming urge to resolve the uneasiness by sharing the full truth with him, so I launched into the story.

My choice not to use complicated or long words started nine years earlier, in my first year of college. During my freshman year I was coming straight out of a six-year stint in an exclusive, academically rigorous, all-girls boarding school. The school was a K-12 with only a handful of boarding students in the upper grades, of which my sister and I were a part. At our boarding school, smart was cool and nobody thought anything about it.

We all loved learning and all basked in the joy of language. We would get lost in the dictionary when we had to look up words. Latin and French weren't elective courses for us, but mandatory parts of our curriculum starting as early as fifth grade. In the 11th and 12th grades our only elective—which very few of the girls elected *not* to take—was Greek. So over the course of the years we had all acquired extensive vocabularies enriched by the study of classical and foreign languages.

It was delightful and was something that all of us at boarding school had taken for granted.

We all used big words and liked it!

When I got to college, I quickly realized that I (and my fellow students from my high school) hadn't actually been the norm. We were pretty nerdy. In fact, my first two years at college were far easier than my last two years of high school.

And, while I may have been academically and linguistically ahead of my college peers, I was socially behind.

Since my school had been an all-girls school, I hadn't been in a classroom with boys since the sixth grade. Not even once. Never! I had had a few male teachers in those six years, but no male peers. We didn't have joint dances or social events. We were strictly forbidden to fraternize and risked expulsion if we got caught socializing with boys outside of a family environment without a chaperone. And, to make matters worse, I wasn't just a day student who had to abide by school rules during the day and went home to a naturally co-ed environment in the evening, I was a boarding student and I lived at the school, with girls and the nuns, for nine out of 12 months a year, for a full six years.

It doesn't take a vivid imagination to get a picture of just how awkward and full of teenage angst I was in a co-ed classroom those first few months of college classes. I was often distracted, wondering if I should or shouldn't look at the boy sitting next to me, take notes in front of him, smile, chat, heck, even breathe! So, it was a good thing I was ahead of the game academically and had solid study habits to help me bridge the gap.

Despite my struggle to adjust to a new social environment, I was then, as I am now, a friendly, outgoing, extroverted person and I wanted a wide friend group. I did make some really great friends and, yes, eventually, even befriended a few of the guys too, but while I made good friends, I wasn't part of the in-crowd, the popular mix of people.

It nettled me not to be among the popular students because, in high school, I had been popular, well-liked, well-respected. Remember that for us, smarts had equaled status and I graduated valedictorian!

For all of those reasons, and more, college was a bit bumpy for the first few months.

And then midterms happened.

Midterm prep was something I had never experienced before. My high school didn't do tests like that. We were expected to be ready for a test at any time in any subject, so we stayed up on our studies consistently and didn't have a feast-and-famine study method. When midterms rolled around, I was a little nervous because of the newness of it all and because of the general anxiety floating around campus, but I wasn't terribly stressed about the content. I had attended every lecture, had taken extensive notes, and had read every single page of assigned reading. I knew the subject matter in all my courses inside and out. I felt ready, and I was open about it.

My peers were not prepared.

At all.

So, in the matter of a few days, I went from being a sideliner to being invited to every study group and every gathering of all the coolest kids in all of my classes. People were preparing for tests 100% of the time and I was a big part of their preparations. I was so sought-after. It was flattering and it stroked my ego which had been bruised over the first few rough months.

It felt great to be invited to those late-night study groups off campus, to be called to join in an impromptu gathering in the student lounge, to compare class notes, to be asked to help prep answers to the study guide.

I loved it. I was all about it!

I felt I had finally made it.

I was in.

I was part of the popular crowd.

Despite my awkwardness around the boys earlier in the year, I had still been incredibly diligent. My boarding school foundations served me well and I helped everyone prepare to rock and ace their exams. I gave out copies of my notes and I helped people study and prepare. And they got good grades. We all did.

I was so happy for all of my new-found (popular) friends and, although super awkward and uncomfortable with going, I was delighted to be asked to a post-midterms, off-campus party to celebrate our successes. There were kids from other schools and drinking and loud music and the house we went to was packed with college kids. I felt uncomfortable and out of place. I quietly slipped out early after I lost track of the friends who had invited me.

I may not have loved the party or even have enjoyed myself much while I was there, but I did love the invitation.

I loved being included.

It made me feel accepted and seen.

And I couldn't wait for the next one.

When classes resumed, I kept waiting and waiting. I had felt that the people who had invited me to all of their study groups and I were now friends. I truly expected them to treat me the way they had during exam prep: to invite me to their gatherings, to keep me in the loop on things that were going on, to include me.

And they didn't.

Nobody called.

Nobody reached out.

Not one invitation to a casual gathering, a late-night coffee, or even to join them in the cafeteria for dinner came. Not a text. Not a call. Nothing.

It stung.

I had so wanted to be known and to be liked for the person that I was and that didn't seem to be the case. They liked me because I was smart. They liked me because I had something to offer to them—information and answers to prep-guide study-questions and, most of all, meticulous notes from every lecture in every class I was in. I was a great study partner. A great tutor.

But not friend material.

I was still in the process of calibrating my social compass and adjusting to a totally new social environment and this was all really hard for me to accept.

I felt so hurt and so used.

Being wanted because I was intelligent was particularly painful to me at that stage of my life because I had truly wanted to be liked for all of who I was, not just for my smarts.

It took me quite a few weeks to get over my hurt feelings and, when the pain subsided, I made a decision. Never again would I put myself in a position to be liked because I was smart. In fact, I didn't even want to appear to be smart. I wanted to be average. I wanted to be like everyone else and to be liked, loved, pursued for who I was as a person, not for how smart I was or for how incredible my notes were.

At the time, I didn't see being smart as part of who I was at the core, and I didn't want anyone to know that I was smart anymore.

It was then that I decided to adjust my vocabulary. I made a decision to give up big, long, multisyllabic words. I was going to keep my language a little less brainy and a lot more normal. I also made the decision never again to share my grades with anyone in my class.

They were promises I made to myself, rules I set in stone, internally. I had never breathed a word about them to anyone at all—not even to myself—but I was telling the story now.

And I told him that I had stuck to both promises religiously with only one exception.

When I was hanging out with my sister (she was two years ahead of me at the same college) and her friends late at night, studying or just relaxing, and we would start to get loopy from lack of sleep, we would whip out our biggest, longest, most atypical multisyllabic words. The longer the words, the better. We would laugh and be intentionally silly about it. We would try to one-up each other with more and more obscure words. Her friends thought it was hilarious and would tell us that when the MacRae girls start using those big words, we all know it's well past bedtime.

Her friends would joke about it. Mine never got the chance because I never did it around them.

But that was it.

In the second half of my first semester in college, nine years before the moment in the garage, I had made a conscious effort not to appear to be smart by adhering strictly to my rule never to use long or complicated words.

When that whole angsty story had come pouring out, and I had bared a big, vulnerable piece of myself, my would-be boyfriend sort of chuckled and asked me, "Are you *really* serious about the vocabulary thing?"

I told him I was and added, again, "I don't want people to know that I'm smart."

His reply froze me.

"Madeleine. Anyone who has had more than a five-minute conversation with you knows that you're smart."

I could not believe it. That simply couldn't be true. I thought I was hiding it so well.

How could everyone know?

It was my turn to ask him if *he* was serious. By his tone, I could tell that he was as surprised by all of this as I was, but we were standing on totally separate sides of the equation.

I was sitting there, still in my car, in shock. It was like I was the emperor in the old folk tale of the Emperor's New Clothes, walking confidently down the street in what I thought were gorgeous garments, hiding that part of me that I wanted hidden, only to find out that I was totally stark-naked waltzing down the street in absolutely nothing.

Exposed.

Nothing was covered or hidden after all.

He was sitting in his Miami condo feeling like he was stating the obvious.

And, with one simple sentence, he had shifted my whole paradigm and had made me aware that, no matter what I did, I wasn't hiding the smart part of me. It was so much of who I was—who I am—that there wasn't anything I could do to conceal it.

We had a really great debrief about the whole thing and while he and I never did become an official item, he gave me a great gift that day. He made me realize that when something is an essential part of who you are, it cannot be hidden or disguised—at least not forever.

In the words of the bard himself, William Shakespeare, "truth will out."

That whole conversation was exposing, but it was liberating too.

The year was 2010.

By that phase of my life, I was already living a strengths-forward existence. I had long since given up looking for and focusing on my weaknesses and my insufficiencies and had turned the eyes of my inner self to my talents and skills—my strengths. Four years prior to that jarring but freeing chat in the parking garage of my apartment building, I had read the book *Now, Discover Your Strengths* by Donald O. Clifton and Marcus Buckingham and it fundamentally changed my worldview.

Prior to reading that book, I had spent the majority of my life focused on all the ways in which I wasn't good enough and pouring intense and steady effort into fixing my weaknesses. I remember so vividly cheating on a spelling test in the second grade because, no matter how many times I wrote out the words, no matter how hard I studied them, I just could not get them right on the weekly spelling test. For my high-achieving self, it was torture.

So, I had written the words in pencil on my desk and had slowly copied and erased them one by one as the teacher read them aloud. I aced the test but felt so guilty that I never cheated on another test again—not in my entire life. I never cheated on anyone or anything at all. It made me feel too guilty. I couldn't take it.

But I did study. For years I worked on my spelling. I studied etymology and learned as many spelling hacks as I could. I drilled spelling into my head in any way that I could. And, finally, eight years later, in tenth grade, I was asked by one of my peers how to spell a word and I knew the answer.

Since we studied classical and foreign languages in junior high and high school, the spelling that was hard for me in English was impossible in other languages. Week after week after week I would fail vocabulary quizzes. I would study hard, and I could pass verbally in flying colors. In writing, though, no amount of effort would make an ounce of difference. My teachers knew I was diligent and was doing the work and after realizing that I was putting in the effort without getting any discernible benefit, I was offered the option to hand in a 10x list with my quizzes—a handwritten list of all of my vocabulary words, correctly spelled, written out, with their definitions, ten times each. As long as the spelling was correct on all ten lines across all of the vocabulary words, they wouldn't count my poor quiz grade against my average. I took advantage of it every day, in every language. It was a gracious mercy to my GPA.

While spelling was never my gift, ironically, writing was. From the day that I learned how to structure a great composition, I became an avid writer. Week after week, my work would be read aloud (anonymously) to the class as the exemplar of great writing. No matter the subject or the time-crunch, I could craft a great piece with a little bit of elbow grease.

It left me joyful and feeling accomplished even when I had to work hard at it.

I had talent for writing, and I learned the skill I needed to make it a strength.

When I read *Now, Discover Your Strengths*—twice, back-to-back, cover-to-cover, something I very rarely do—I found a new way to look at myself. And my torrid past with spelling made the point that Clifton and Buckingham were making in their book abundantly clear to me: when you devote your time to your weaknesses, it's a draining process that yields inconsistent, slow results and leaves you feeling less-than all the time. Whereas when you focus on your strengths, you go twice as far in half the time and are left feeling better and more capable than ever.

I hadn't ever considered my strengths until that point. I hadn't genuinely asked myself what I was good at beyond writing. I had only really looked for what I wasn't good at.

After reading that book, I decided that I was worth getting to know.

I started by taking the Clifton Strengths Finder™—an assessment that came with the book. It categorizes your strengths from strongest to least strong and helps you interpret how they show up for you in your professional life. Their advice was that you focus on your top ten traits and hyper-focus on your top five. Truth be told, I hardly recognized myself in the assessment results the first time I took the test. I accepted that my top strengths were an accurate reflection of me, but there were only a few components that truly resonated. I couldn't see them as clearly as I do in hindsight.

The assessment said that my greatest strength was Activator, and they said that I succeed using my Activator strength because "you are a catalyst... Your energy can be contagious and engaging." I didn't feel that I was using that strength in any way whatsoever and it felt very foreign to me, but it stuck with me and, as I pondered it more and more over the course of months and years, I started to see its threads woven into the fabric of my life for as far back as I could remember.

Even when I was a tiny kid, I could easily get people to listen to me and to do what I suggested. It wasn't hard and wasn't something that I needed to work for, so I had overlooked it and had taken it for granted as something that was common and that everyone could probably do.

That couldn't be further from the truth. Not everyone has that catalytic quality.

And there was one story that jumped out at me from my childhood that bore that out.

It was a summer afternoon in the early years of elementary school. It was the latter half of the '80s. My brother, my sister, and I were gathered with a few of our friends at our house. My mom was in the house while all of us were playing outside. We had spent hours swimming, riding bikes, and hanging out and were resting in the shade of the garage.

We had been playing for a long time and were discussing what we should do next.

There was a sort of unsettled feeling in our tight-knit group, and we all sensed more than understood that if there wasn't a solid idea of what to do next, everyone would be done for the day and head home.

I didn't want that.

I wanted to keep playing and so did everyone else—there just wasn't one unifying idea to pull us all together.

Everyone wanted to do something a little different and there was the hum of voices as idea after idea got offered to the group. Let's go back in the pool: shot down. Nobody wanted to get dressed and undressed again. Let's roller skate downstairs in the house: that was a no-go, Mom had told us we had to stay outside and play.

Ideas were popping like popcorn, but none of them were good enough to stick.

I was on the fringe of the circle, just listening to all of the ideas and objecting if I really disliked an idea, but most of all, I was quietly taking it all in as I so often do. I am rarely the one to come up with the best or the most innovative idea out of the blue. I'm the person who spots a good idea and becomes its champion or who builds off of a fantastic start.

And that's exactly what happened here.

The suggestions were continuing to flow.

One of our friends suggested a bike ride around the block. We had already done that. Another person suggested a game of freeze tag. That didn't seem like a terrible idea, but nobody else leapt at the offer. My sister suggested that we go to the park up the street and play. That seemed like a good idea, but nobody really latched onto it either. A few other people threw out a few final hail-Mary ideas: hopscotch, jump rope, foursquare. Nothing really compelling came out of the brainstorm session—well at least, nothing as good as my sister's suggestion to go to the park.

People were starting to get a little restless and I could tell we were seconds away from everyone going home. *That* wasn't going to happen, so I piped up a very strong endorsement of the best idea that anyone had had yet, and I said, "You know, let's go to the park!"

Everyone erupted with a huge resounding chorus of yesses: "Yeah! Let's go to the park." "That sounds like fun." "Great idea." My sister was annoyed because it had been her idea and nobody wanted to do it then but just because I suggested it, suddenly it was a great idea. I knew it had been her idea and I wasn't trying to take credit for the idea. I just wanted to keep playing, so I turned to her and said, "Yeah, I know. And it was a great idea. So, let's go."

Someone ran into the house to tell mom that we were heading to the park.

The rest of us scrambled into the garage to get our bikes.

My one little suggestion had taken our group from acting like a hive of drowsy, lazy bees to a unified swarm ready to buzz away.

In minutes the whole pack of us were biking down tree-lined suburban streets headed to the park, ready to have a great time in the late afternoon sun, exploring the woods, swinging on swings, enjoying the simple joys of childhood and friendship.

It was just that simple.

I didn't try. I didn't have to persuade. I didn't even offer any compelling reasons why I thought the park idea was the best. I just heard the idea, thought it was the best one and shouted it out. Everyone got on board.

Turns out, I was a catalyst, an Activator.

My sister is not.

We do not all have the same gifts, talents, inclinations, strengths.

And, while I didn't see it at first, it is true that I'm an Activator to my very core. I have always been one and will always be one.

It is part of who I am.

As I delved into my strengths more and more, it was exciting to have some language to express things that I had vaguely known about myself and to put some focus on growing parts of me that were already naturally strong.

At the same time, it was intimidating not to see myself in so much of what the assessment had said my genuine and greatest strengths were. That wasn't ok for me. I wanted to see myself more fully, more completely, so I became a student of myself.

I sought to understand how I ticked, what gifts I really had and to see how they could be strengthened and put to productive use. As time went on, I saw my strengths in myself more and more. I no longer looked for my deficiencies and my issues. Of course, I took care not to let my weaknesses be or become liabilities and I built good strong bridges over the worst of them, but I looked towards my gifts and found ways to grow them, to hone them and to use them.

I've taken the Clifton Strengths Finder™ assessment three times in my life. The first one, in 2006 right after reading the book and at the very onset of my professional career, the second time in 2011 at the peak of my corporate career, and then in 2019 well into my entrepreneurial journey. The coolest thing about it has been the relative lack of change in my core strengths and my core weaknesses. While I only saw a small glimmer of my own reflection in the first set of results, the last set of results was a very accurate reflection of who I am both in strengths and weaknesses—and they were well-nigh identical to the first time.

The results didn't change.

I did.

I had become aware of my strengths and had consciously worked to develop them. I was rooted in an appreciation of who I was and who I am and whether people liked me or not did not determine the course of my actions. Of course, I still prefer to be liked, included, appreciated as much now as I did in college, but what other people see and think about me isn't as relevant or as important to me as it was back then. Since I now know and like myself, the external validation is far less impactful to me.

My appreciation of my gifts, my awareness of my own strengths, my acceptance of my weaknesses isn't contingent on someone else. It all stands on its own and I don't need to cower or to hide. I don't need to hide the best and brightest parts of myself or to excuse and avoid the weakest parts. They are all equally part of me. Neither good nor bad. Just different components of the full reality of who I am.

I recognize that I may not be to everyone's liking, I may not be invited to the table with the popular people, my smarts might make me weird or unrelatable. And that's all ok.

I don't allow the limited way that someone else might perceive me to define me. I don't need the external validation of others because I know that I have—as every single person on the face of the planet has—something special and unique to offer.

My strengths may not be the same as yours. You may never have enjoyed the flight of inspiration as your fingers danced over the keys of a keyboard. You may never have spoken in front of a big crowd or led a team of people or built a business through the sheer force of your will.

And that's ok.

You are a beautiful, unique, compelling expression of specific talents and skills and strengths and weaknesses that are trying to be seen and understood, to be loved and appreciated, to be utilized and enjoyed. And if you're reading this book, it means you're serious about that and I applaud you for it.

There is no investment that you could make that would yield a more robust return than an investment in understanding and appreciating and loving who you are. All of who you are.

You are wealthy in so many ways. I have no doubt whatsoever.

Decide to find those inner riches.

They are there if you but look.

EXPLORING WHO YOU ARE

♥

Sometimes it's hard to see ourselves clearly—not because we're unwilling, but because we can't see the picture when we're in the frame.

That is why I love assessments.

Assessments provide well-researched and specific insights that allow you to see yourself from a different angle. I took my first one at sixteen and have done tons of them throughout my life and my career. As a business coach, I encourage my clients to use assessments, profiles, tests and I want to encourage you to use them too!

The more circumspectly and the more deeply you understand yourself, the better.

Do a little digging and find an assessment* that aligns with an area that you're interested to know more about: core strengths, external perception, communication style, decision making and management... Clifton StrengthsFinder™ is my go-to recommendation, but just pick one that resonates with you.

Do the assessment. Take the time to truly sit with the results.

Trace your way back to specific instances in your life where you showed up in the way that the results indicate. Get specific with it and see yourself as fully as you can. If any of your memories are shrouded in doubt or worry or disempowering narratives, get some help to transform them, to see them with fresh eyes.

If you're hesitant to look more closely, anxious that you'll be underwhelmed with what you find out about yourself, I would highly recommend that you start by reading *Now, Discover Your Strengths* by Donald O. Clifton and Marcus Buckingham. We all have strengths. All of us. And discovering mine changed my life. It might just help you to change yours too!

---

*Assessments to explore: Myers-Briggs Type Indicator, Fascinate Test, DiSC assessment, Predictive Index and Clifton StrengthsFinder™.

CHAPTER 3

KNOW WHERE YOU ARE

"The world breaks everyone and afterwards
many are strong at the broken places."

— ERNEST HEMINGWAY

I STEPPED INTO MY THIRTIES AT THE TOP OF MY GAME.

I WAS IN THE BEST SHAPE of my life physically and emotionally. I had a fantastic career as a corporate executive. I was financially stable, professionally successful, living in a gorgeous mid-rise apartment in the heart of downtown Philadelphia.

I was thriving.

Fast-forward a couple of years and my life was hardly recognizable.

I had relinquished my power and found myself unintentionally living in a tragic and disempowering storyline.

As had happened earlier in my life, I had gotten into a relationship that had a deeply negative impact on my life. While many people learn hard lessons, stumble and are forced to grow through professional or academic challenges, the biggest and most painful lessons of the early stages of my adult life happened in my personal life—primarily in my relationships.

This time, I had fallen in love with someone who loved the idea of me, but who didn't truly love me.

I only saw it after the fact, but he had deep wounds in his soul and, in an effort to ameliorate his own pain, he would spread the pain around through emotional manipulation and deeply diminishing behaviors. His emotionally abusive ways were seldom blatant or overt and, while others may have observed them, I wasn't aware of them and I would venture to bet that he wasn't either.

When I first met Paul, I really liked him. He was smart, tall and charming. He had a business that he was dedicated to growing, kids whom he loved but was separated from, and lots of drama to contend with. It seemed he had gotten the raw end of the deal on several fronts and was going through a really rough patch in his life.

My compassionate heart wanted to help him through the stormy seas, wanted to help him thrive.

Little did I know that the rough patch would be ever evolving and that those seas would nearly drown me.

The unraveling of our relationship took place over a long period of time and a wide range of circumstances, but my final decision to leave the relationship was solidified one morning around Thanksgiving minutes after we had had a huge and stunning fight about money.

Paul and I started our relationship on fairly equal financial footing. I had worked hard to become debt free years prior to dating him and he had debts of every sort: alimony, child support, medical school debt, and his car. So while our monthly earnings were not the same, our take-home was similar and our financial power dynamic was fairly well balanced.

He was just getting out of a 16-year marriage where he had used money as a form of control. But for the majority of our relationship, when he tried to initiate fights with me on the basis of money, I had been able to pull out my checkbook and settle the issue with the stroke of a pen, if needed. So, firing that type of ammunition at me had been consistently unsuccessful.

I had a great job at a solid company with a fantastic compensation plan and didn't need or want his money.

But, after the birth of our son, I gave up that job for a plethora of reasons—one of which was to help Paul build his business. It was doing well at the time and we had plans to expand it and make it something truly significant.

He wanted me to help him prepare to scale.

It was the perfect role for me and I was more than happy to help him make that happen despite having to take over a 70% pay cut to do it.

He had agreed to pay the lion's share of our living expenses. I knew his growing business couldn't handle the corporate salary and bonuses I was used to, and I saw myself building this asset with him, so the salary wasn't terribly important to me at the time. I said yes to helping him formalize and bring a dynamic growth plan to life.

I got to it right away and brought systems and processes to his business. It was fun for a while, but working together was not healthy for us. We had vastly different management styles and he kept cutting me down and undermining me in the business. I couldn't tolerate that professionally—although I seemed to allow it personally—and I ended up pulling back significantly from my role within his organization less than two months after formally giving up my corporate career. I continued to support, in an administrative and accounting capacity, and to help with the bigger strategic things remotely, but I was no longer involved in the day-to-day of the business. We cut my salary even further, but kept a token amount on the books as a nod to my ongoing work.

I started to pursue other interests while taking care of my son and still working part time on the business.

Six weeks after our working situation shifted, his business was hit with a devastating legal situation. It was huge and unexpected and hit him out of left field. It left the business in extreme financial distress and both Paul and I were shaken to the quick.

Revenue dried up.

While I no longer had my corporate job, I did have a nest egg we could lean on. I wanted to help our little family survive the upheaval, so I transferred all our personal payments—even his most personal ones—to my accounts and I agreed to suspend my salary too.

The business was financially stressed for a little longer than I had anticipated, and my nest egg dwindled to more like a fish egg than the big ostrich egg it had once been.

It was stressful and scary.

When the initial wave was over and things got on firmer footing again, we shifted his expenses back to his accounts and had a chat about renewing my salary. We mutually agreed to continue it where it had been before the troubles cropped up because of what I had just done to help, and because I was still putting in a ton of work every day.

We talked numbers openly. He knew where I was financially and he knew that I didn't want my financial safety net to get any smaller. My salary from my work with his business kept me at net zero impact—no gain, no loss—and let me contribute what had once been my fair share, but was now my full income's share, to our living expenses.

Things were at a status quo again. Not a very comfortable one for me, but at least a stable one and that was a welcome change.

The financial stress abated mildly.

Until the morning of our fight.

It erupted entirely out of the blue.

Paul found a pay stub from his company for me on our kitchen counter. He stormed into my office, paper-in-hand, and slapped it on my desk. I had been quietly working on his business bookkeeping and it startled me.

He stood right in front of my desk, pulled himself to his full 6'2" height and started to get loud.

He was acting like I had stolen from him. He started talking as if this small sum of money was something he knew nothing about. And he demanded to see where he authorized this salary at all.

He said that when I stopped coming into the office I should have stopped being paid.

He called me a thief, a liar, and a cheat.

He berated me and accused me in a way that had me both infuriated and bewildered.

This wasn't the first time he had made me question myself, wonder if maybe I was the one who understood it all wrong, who remembered incorrectly. His manipulations were so subtle and so persistent that I hardly noticed them on a day-to-day basis and when we fought, he would reap the fruits of the doubts he had sown. He made accusations that pushed through the spaces where his constant criticisms had eroded the confidence that once used to fill that space so strongly.

I could feel it, but I couldn't see it or name it at that stage.

I was so fixated on the accusation that I wasn't paying attention to anything else. It was like a storm was happening around me but he was ringing this tiny little bell that had one hundred percent of my focus and attention. I had to silence the bell.

And the only way I could silence this specific bell, today, was with tangible proof.

But I had no proof.

Our agreement had been verbal, and, since I was handling all the finances and payroll and had simply executed what we discussed, I had no way to disprove his accusations.

He flatly denied having ever authorized keeping my salary, much less renewing it. And, on top of that, he acted like it was some huge sum when it was less than the part-time salary of even his most junior team member.

I was flustered and feverishly scrolling through our texts and searching my email while he imposingly settled himself into the chair across from me separated only by my desk and a wall of ice and fire.

No matter how hard I looked, I couldn't find one shred of evidence that I was right and he demanded that I terminate my payroll at that moment.

Like a beaten animal, I silently logged in to the account and, with the click of just a few boxes, formally unemployed myself and terminated any future payments.

He then demanded proof that some of the personal expenses I had recently made—like hiring a health coach—came out of my own accounts and not out of his.

I pulled up all the data he wanted to see.

In that, at least, I could defend myself.

He couldn't catch me in a lie or prove that I was taking his money because I wasn't.

I had had access to his money for over two years at this point, personally and professionally. I knew every login, every account number, every password. And I had never once taken a single cent without his knowledge or authorization. I had never used his money as mine.

The thought had never even crossed my mind.

My personal integrity is sacrosanct to me.

He knew that and he attacked it.

I was shell-shocked.

The professional issue was already bad, but this more proximate personal attack made it exponentially worse.

I had just spent nearly every cent that I had so carefully saved for years to keep his business, our life and our family afloat, and here he was treating me like a criminal. If I had intended to steal there were a thousand less obvious ways I could have gone about it than putting my own salary back on payroll. Pointing out all of that did nothing.

His position was firm.

He would not be swayed.

It went on for a long time and eventually my defiance and anger resolved into a defeated silence. There was nothing more for me to say.

He refused to believe me.

He refused to acknowledge conversations and agreements that we had had many times. He was gaslighting me, and it was working.

I was fading.

He stormed out of the house, jumped in his car and sped off who knows where. He was gone the rest of the day.

Noah was sleeping peacefully upstairs.

I was alone with my thoughts.

I stood there, in the middle of the living room, dazed, looking around but seeing nothing.

As my senses slowly came back to me, I started to wander around the first floor of the house aimlessly. With each step the reality of the hurtfulness of his accusations seeped in deeper and deeper. As my feet went from the smooth hardwood floors to the plush carpet, I was internally stunned by how committed he was to his false narrative, his lies.

I was shocked that he chose to believe that I had lapsed so heinously in integrity.

It was like he didn't know me at all.

It hurt.

So much.

I felt like I just couldn't take it for another second and I crumbled to the floor in a heap of overwhelm and tears.

Mini versions of this scenario had been happening for a long time and that day, that fight, felt like it pulled my spine right out of my back.

I felt worthless.

Defeated.

Invisible.

I cried there on the floor for a good long time. By the time the tears were all cried out, I was utterly exhausted. I could hardly lift my head from the carpet. I was reclining in child's pose to try to calm myself. My head was resting on the carpet. The waffle pattern was imprinted on my forehead.

And then my phone rang. It was one of my dearest friends and I answered with a strained hello.

She heard it in my voice immediately.

"What's wrong? What's going on? Have you been crying?" she asked in a shocked tone.

The whole humiliating narrative came pouring out of me in one long, flowing answer. I didn't leave anything out. Not even the exact dollar amounts. She knew what I had been making in my corporate role and I could tell she was shocked by the number.

Silence.

I knew she was there, but she wasn't saying a word.

It was like the line had gone dead.

Now, this friend isn't shy. She says what she feels, and you always know where you stand with her. She will call you out when you're not being your best self and will support you to the ends of the earth too. But she is a friend who never, and I mean in over a dozen years of friendship, never, ever weighed in on any of my relationship stuff. She always had my back but always let me figure things out on my own without her bias impacting me. She feels it is not her place and she doesn't want to damage the friendships she holds dear, so she keeps her thoughts to herself.

This was an exception.

A big one.

I was beginning to second-guess having shared so much with her. The money issues with Paul had been uncomfortable since way before his business troubles had started. He had always tried to manipulate me with money, but I had always had plenty to thwart his efforts... until now.

Our relationship hadn't been terribly strong before and now things were more than rocky. We were distant and it had been so hard. We had tried therapy and he made it so uncomfortable. He had misrepresented our relationship to the therapist, and it made matters worse. I went back and worked on myself. He didn't.

I hadn't told her much about it before.

I hadn't really told anyone outside of my parents.

I had kept it all very close and very private.

I felt ashamed that my relationship was falling apart, that I had given up my career, my financial security, my freedom; that I had hitched my wagon to his without anything binding us together.

There was no ring.

There was no contract.

There was a child. And that was an important, key piece, but it wasn't the same as a commitment.

And yet I had given everything I had to give.

All of those thoughts were pulsating through my aching and groggy head during those few seconds—which felt to me like decades—of silence.

I was still in a dark sort of haze from everything that had just transpired, and I thought she was going to discreetly defer to answer, say something to make me feel better, and comfort me.

That is not what happened.

"Maddie, what are you doing? Seriously, what in the heck are you doing?"

It was like a bolt of lightning went through my body and zapped me out of the fog I had been living in for months. And, at the same time, I felt like a bucket of cold water had been splashed on my face and I suddenly jolted out of a nightmarish dream to a state of being fully awake, aware, and energized.

My eyes got really wide.

My head cleared.

I stood up from the floor.

She continued, and I listened with my mouth agape.

"This man should be treating you like a princess. You are taking care of his children, and his home, and his business. You sacrificed your career; you bought a house for him; you moved to his location. You have given him years of your time. The best years you have to give. And now this? You've sacrificed your financial security too?

"And he's not your fiancée. He's not your husband.

"He. Is. Your. Boyfriend. That's it.

"You are the mother of his child. He should be taking care of you and making you feel loved and safe and supported and cherished. And, instead, *this* is what has been going on?

"*What* are you doing?"

She continued to say that she had had reservations for a long time. She had always seen his narcissistic traits, but she assumed that he was good to me. She assumed that he was taking good care of me in all ways—especially financially. She knew what I had given up, had sacrificed, and she thought those sacrifices were being honored on his side.

She made it clear that she could not support me continuing on like this.

She talked about what a savvy businesswoman I am. She reminded me of my accomplishments, my smarts, my passion for life, and my magnetism towards success. She detailed just how much I had to offer and what a strong, capable person I was.

She lifted a mirror up to show me the incredible woman I was—a woman who had somehow been shrouded under the weight of shame and worry and fear.

I stood there, gazing out the window, looking over the top of the trees growing on the steep slope of our lot, soaking it all in, feeling alive again in a way that I hadn't felt in many, many months.

Seeing myself again.

She talked about what I needed to do, the actions I needed to take. She felt it was time for me to leave.

She told me I deserved so much better.

And for the first time in just as many months, I believed that I did too.

That day, that conversation, that one rhetorical question, asked with urgency and deliberate pace and emphasis, "What in the heck are you doing?" had done the trick. I knew I had to leave. I knew I had lost myself and it was high time to stop acting like I had no choice but to stay.

I had been unhappy for months—profoundly unhappy—and my parents had seen it. They knew I had given up my independence and that the house I had bought wasn't mine alone. And they had offered me a soft place to land. They told me that my son and I were welcome to come and stay with them for as long as I needed to get back on my feet. They knew my position and they didn't judge me or make me feel small or bad about it.

They just offered their help and waited for me to be ready to say yes to it.

I had never let them help me before—not after I was in a big car accident many years earlier, not after my first disastrous relationship had wreaked havoc on my life a decade prior—never. I had always looked at asking for or accepting their support in much the same way as I had looked upon therapy so many years earlier—as a failure of myself. But that wasn't what it was. It was a gift being freely given to me with no strings attached.

A gift of love.

And this conversation with my dear friend helped me to see that I deserved to be loved, to be supported, to be given a steady hand to support my wobbly legs as I got up from the ground where I had too often found myself, prostrate, crying and feeling broken.

I had been trapped in a tragic storyline and at this moment, I realized that the time was now to say yes to a new, more empowered, and more empowering narrative.

It took me a couple of months to exit kindly and respectfully. Paul and I decided to make my departure a break rather than a break-up, and I was at home in Michigan being cherished and supported by my mom and dad, with my sweet little son, a week before Christmas. Noah was 16 months old.

That was the beginning of my transition out of the tragic storyline I had unintentionally slid into. But that wasn't quite the end of the saga.

When I got to Michigan, Paul started acting even more strangely. I had a suspicion that something was going to implode. I didn't know what it was, but I could feel it brewing and I hired a coach to support me just in case.

And I was right.

There was a storm brewing.

On New Year's Eve, I was awakened from a deep sleep by an alarm on my phone. I keep my phone beside my bed but on silent at night, so the sound jolted me awake. It was the security system on my house in Pennsylvania. The external security cameras had been triggered. It was three in the morning. I groggily opened the app and there she was, standing in plain view of the camera, smoking a cigarette—his receptionist, twenty-five years his junior.

My mind raced to find a justifiable reason for her to be there. I went from a sleepy, half-awake state to wide awake. My mind was playing out scenarios, my stomach was churning. I knew his kids were there, so maybe something happened with them. In my gut, I knew what was going on but I didn't want to see it. I didn't want to jump to any conclusions without more information. We had decided to go on a break, not to fully break up, so I was feeling confused and upset. If he wanted to be with someone else, he could have just ended things with me.

I was unsettled and upset. I searched through every video the system had saved, I tried to find more information, but there wasn't anything else. He had turned off the interior cameras and I couldn't see what was going on. The cameras only triggered when there was atypical movement.

I felt unsatisfied, but it was the dead of night still and I needed to sleep. I ripped myself away from my phone and decided to wait until the morning to do anything about it.

I slipped back into a fitful sleep.

I woke up early the next day. I didn't say a word to my mom or dad, and I privately reached out to Paul's ex-wife. We were on cordial terms, and I knew that their kids would be returning from their holiday break with their dad soon—if they weren't already back. I told her what had happened the night before and she said she would let me know what the kids had to say about it. We both knew that if there was something going on between their dad and his receptionist, they would say something to their mom.

The next day, she confirmed my worst fears.

Paul and his receptionist were in a relationship.

Suddenly, all the puzzle pieces fell into place.

I finally understood what had been happening over the past eight months. He had already moved onto a new relationship. That terrible couple-therapy session with him, his sudden leaving from the house, his hurry back home when we were on a family vacation—all of it made sense with that one critical piece of information in place. The picture of our failed relationship was so clear, so suddenly obvious to me.

I was infuriated.

I felt so betrayed, hurt, angry.

Noah was napping and I walked into the kitchen, sat down at the table, and told my mom everything. I was about to turn into a puddle crying on the living room floor again when I heard the voice of my coach in my head, "If something happens, call me. If you feel like you shouldn't bother me, call me. If you feel like you want to get through something on your own, call me." His model was interventional, and he felt he could be of greatest service in the moment whatever thing it was was actually happening.

I told my mom that I needed to call him. She offered to watch Noah if he woke up and I made the call.

I didn't want to do it.

But I knew I needed to do it.

And I'm so glad I did.

I walked downstairs, took a few deep breaths and dialed his number. He answered immediately and the story came pouring out—from the alarm on my phone to the conversation with his ex-wife to my sudden awareness of why things had been so terribly bad over the past many months. All that I could say over and over again was, "Why did he do this to me?" "How could he have done this to me?"

My coach let me vent and then his work started with one bold statement.

"He didn't do this *to you*, he did this *for himself*."

I had been pacing back and forth over the brown and cream tiles—the tiles we had roller-skated on as kids, ran across thousands of times. I was in the middle of a stride when he made that statement. Mid-step, I looked down at my foot. It seemed to have gone into slow motion.

I watched my foot land halfway between a cream and brown tile. My toes were on the cream, my heel was on the brown. I stood rooted there in stunned silence.

And then he repeated, "He didn't do this *to you*, he did this *for himself*."

We were both silent for a moment and time felt like it was still moving at half speed. My tears began to fall silently down my face. And he continued to talk. I don't remember what he said until the words, "He wasn't thinking about you at all. He was only thinking about himself," kicked me back into real-time and I found my voice again.

"But that's exactly the problem," I interrupted, "I *should* have mattered to him. I gave up so much for him. I did so much for him. I took care of him, of our home, his kids, our son. I made his life easy.

I sacrificed so much to make it work. *I should have mattered.* I should have been considered. He should have thought of me"

I was animated, angry, nearly shouting.

"Yes," he answered calmly, "you feel you should have, but you weren't. You feel he should have considered you, but he didn't. The thing is that this wasn't about you. It was about him. It had absolutely nothing to do with you.

"Paul is emotionally drowning and he's doing what drowning people do—they cling to whatever is floating by, and they pull themselves up on it. If it starts to sink or to drown, they don't stop out of care, they only stop to jump to something more buoyant. They don't drag you down because they are cruel or malicious or calculating. They do it because they are drowning. He is drowning and he's doing whatever it takes for him to suck air into his lungs. He's not doing this to hurt you. He's doing this to emotionally save himself."

With each word, my anger diminished slightly, and, by the end of his response, I was calmer and a little bit more receptive to the point that he was making.

And then he asked me to imagine this story.

He told me to imagine that I was at a beautiful resort with some friends. A few of them were going to relax at the pool and a few others, myself included, were going to head out to dinner. I was ready early and wandered down to the pool to spend some time with my friends who wouldn't be joining us for dinner.

I was looking gorgeous.

They were sitting by the pool, with their loungers facing into the sunset, back to the pool.

I pulled up a lounger beside them and we were having an amazing conversation. I wasn't dressed for the pool, but I was loving the sunset and the company and the connection.

And then I was splashed.

I looked over at my friend and made a face, but we just kept on chatting. It wasn't that big of a deal. We were by the pool after all.

We were settling back into the flow of our conversation when another splash came. The second one was more irritating and a little more wet than the first.

I stopped in the middle of my sentence, looked over at them, rolled my eyes and said, "What a jerk!" We all grimaced at each other, shrugged our shoulders and just picked up where we had been so rudely interrupted.

It was a good conversation, no need to ruin it.

Surely it wouldn't happen again.

And then it did.

The third and biggest splash of all came up and soaked my back. Now I was truly angry, and I was going to march over to the side of that pool and give that inconsiderate jerk a piece of my mind. He was going to regret his bad manners.

I swung my feet around to the side of my chair, stood up and stepped to the edge of the pool.

And that's when I saw it: he was drowning.

I was so invested in the story, I had truly imagined myself doing every single thing that my coach described as he described it and the instant he said, "He was drowning," my heart skipped a beat.

He asked me, "What happened to all your anger just now?" And I replied, "It melted."

"Yes," he said, "because he's drowning."

Now, encountering a drowning person does not require that you jump in the water and save them, especially when they are drowning in a shallow pool and could simply stand up. In life, drowning is a choice and once made, it runs your life in a way you don't even realize. But you always, always, have the power to stand back up.

Always.

The point was clear, and I could feel my anger with Paul starting to abate. I wasn't over it yet because I still felt that he should have considered me before he made the decision to cheat, and I told my coach so.

He told me he had another story he wanted to tell me.

He was going to narrate and I was to imagine myself in the scene again.

Imagine that you had come into a significant amount of money, and you decided to fulfill a dream that you've always had. You had always dreamt of having a big, beautiful home with a gorgeous foyer. The sole point of the foyer was to have a statement piece of art installed so that when people walked in, they would see it and feel inspired and maybe even a little impressed.

You had shopped around for a long while, and found the perfect property. The entry was magnificent; exactly what you wanted. But you were on a cul-de-sac and had only two neighbors.

And then you started to shop for the art. It took a while but you found the exact piece that you wanted. It was sheer perfection. It fit the space beautifully. The styles matched; the vibe was perfect. By the time you moved into the space and had the art installed, your heart was glowing with joy and pride.

You couldn't wait to show it off.

You invited your two neighbors over for an intimate little dinner.

The day of the private little party came, and you were a little bit behind schedule. You were still in the kitchen touching up a few things when the bell rang. So you had your friend, who had come early, answer the door for you.

You were so excited to hear your neighbors ooh and ahh over the art. You could hear them from the foyer—not every word, but enough to catch the sentiment. You were rushing to finish up and get in there soon enough to hear their exact comments, but at least you wouldn't miss the initial impressions from here.

You hadn't told them in advance that this was a private sort of unveiling, but the art was so central, there was no way they could miss it.

You heard the door open, and your friend greet the neighbors.

You were straining to hear.

You thought there would be some acknowledgment of the gorgeous piece.

Nothing.

It was weirdly quiet.

Your mind began to race. In one soul-crushing moment, you suddenly doubted everything. Maybe the art wasn't as gorgeous or impressive as I thought. Maybe it was ugly. Oh. My. Gosh! What if I have the worst taste ever? What if they hate it so much, they are just saying nothing? You were starting to feel really embarrassed and you had just put the last piece in order, so you decided to face the music and walked resolutely but with a quaking inside of your gut over to the foyer.

They were just rounding the corner as you drew nearer and the first thing you saw was the long white guide cane.

They were blind.

They didn't hate your art. They didn't even know it existed. They could not see it. They were blind.

All of your misgivings and worry was for naught.

They were blind.

He told me that Paul was no different. He didn't choose not to see me, choose not to perceive me, he just could not see me because he was blind to me.

I had been sitting on a wicker chair following every word, seeing myself in this little scene. I had felt the churning in my stomach as he went over the worry and the doubts and as soon as the eyes of my imagination saw that white cane, everything vanished in a moment.

The negative emotions about Paul vanished too.

I could see something about him that I hadn't before. I could see him as wounded, drowning, blind. I could see his desperation to be ok, his selfish pursuit of his own needs. And I no longer attached myself to his choices.

In that one moment, I was able to detach my storyline from his.

His decision to cheat was about him, not me.

I walked away from that conversation as a stronger, more resilient woman.

Those two stories jolted me free from the tragic narrative that I had been weaving for a long time. I wasn't a victim, a hapless hanger-on.

I was strong and capable.

I had agency.

I could choose how I wanted to feel and I wanted to be ok.

I wanted to smile like I used to, to feel like myself again.

I wanted to be free.

And so I was.

I could have been a puddle of self-pity and sorrow that day. I could have slipped deeper into a victim mentality and been trapped there for months, even years, but that day the coach I had hired made me see things in a whole new way. I could never have anticipated the impactful nature of his role in my life.

As it turned out, I had to sever personal and professional ties with that coach a few months later, sealing it with a legal action. Despite all of that, I will always be grateful for what he did for me that day.

He was a vessel of transformation for me at a crucial moment in my life story.

He prevented me from slipping further from where I wanted to be, who I wanted to be.

That evening, I found myself laughing and joking with my mom as we casually shopped at our local grocery store. I was skipping, lighthearted, happy.

I remember commenting to her how strange it felt to be that happy, that ok, that relieved after hearing such shocking news that very day. Even on that day, I knew just how big of a deal it was to be where I was, to be genuinely moving in a good direction, standing on solid emotional footing.

It felt almost miraculous.

That day, I chose a more empowering narrative. The cheating wasn't the tragic conclusion of my life story, it was the necessary ending of a hard and painful chapter and the beginning of something new. A new reality where I could choose not to go near the pool when I wasn't in the mood to be splashed.

Our stories are unfolding every single day and it is our privilege—not our punishment—to be able to craft the narrative. Even if you are not where you wished you would be. Even if you have drifted off course or maybe you haven't ever considered the course at all. No matter what, it is essential that you know that you are in charge of your own story.

Where you are in your story is the result of your choices, but it doesn't have to be where you stay forever. In order not to stay stuck where you are, you have to know where you are, accept it, decide to do something differently and then pluck up all your courage and make that first step in a new direction.

After my breakup with Paul, I realized that I was caught in a loop in my life. I had found myself in a repetitive cycle of getting involved with unavailable men and Paul was no different. He was emotionally unavailable, and I decided that he would be the last.

I was fair-minded enough to know that all of this was not 100% his fault. I played my part too. There was something in me that had attracted such a wounded soul. I had called out to him and had wanted to heal him. And I knew that I could make a new decision going forward. I decided to find out what was so wounded in me that had been so drawn to him, and to heal it.

And I embarked on a multi-year journey of intense healing.

I decided that I had agency. And, from this moment onwards, you absolutely must live your life as though you have agency too—because you do.

As though you have worth—because you do.

As though you are exactly where you are supposed to be—because you are.

The only place from which you can chart your course is the exact place where you are in this very moment as you read these very words.

You cannot begin at the place you wish you were.

You must begin where you are because where you are is exactly the right place to begin.

HONORING YOUR GPS

♥

Sometimes I catch myself playing the what-if game. Imagining a future where I stayed in the relationships I chose to leave, where I said no to the promotion that I actually took, where I said yes to the trip I declined to take or the date I didn't go on. I think about what my life would be if I had made other choices, what I would have avoided and what I would have missed out on having.

Our lives are an intricate tapestry of roads not taken and trails unexplored. Of yesses that set off an avalanche of dominoes we could have never imagined. Of delays that sometimes saved our lives.

Just as changing one thread on the warp or the weave makes the whole textile look different, altering one decision along the way changes the look of our lives too.

All of our choices—the ones that make us proud and the ones that don't—have led us to today.

And we have to start where we are.

We are where we are for a reason.

A good reason.

We are here, being served up exactly what we need no matter the wrapping paper.

When we are in a place that we're not at all proud of being, we often want to hide, perhaps even from ourselves. We want to avoid the feelings of guilt or grief or disappointment. But maybe, just maybe when we've had enough of them, those are the very feelings that will propel us onward and upwards.

Don't waste a single moment of your time wishing you were starting somewhere else. You aren't. You are starting here. And even the most sophisticated GPS needs a starting point from which to navigate to a new destination.

And this, right here, right now, today, is the starting point of your new tomorrow.

Where will you choose to go?

Take things deeper at:
www.madeleinemacrae.com/gifts

♡ *Madeleine*

CHAPTER 4

NARRATIVE CONTROL

"You can't go back and change the beginning, but you can start from where you are and change the ending."

— UNKNOWN

THE ROOM WAS COOL.

T HE EVENING CHILL of the Canadian Rockies had settled into the air shortly after sunset.

It had been the first full day of our retreat, and everything had already been so moving. We plumbed the depths of our souls and many of us were still processing what we had found there. It had been nearly nine months since my split with Paul when I had decided to find and heal the wounds within me, and I had been working closely with an incredible coach to support me in this phase of my journey. Her specialty was story, and she had brought together a room full of incredible women who were ready to own their own story.

We had only been together for a little over twenty-four hours at this point; so much had been moving that we were all a bit fatigued. But we were also curious about this seemingly impromptu evening session. It hadn't even been on our agenda and was announced only a few hours earlier at dinner.

So, despite the fatigue, we made the short trek from our cozy, rustic cabins to the central hub of the retreat center and started to gather outside the large room that did dual duty as a yoga studio and meeting space.

Our retreat leader smiled invitingly as we started to file into the softly lit room.

She asked us to enter quietly and get comfy in a wide semicircle around her.

She was sitting peacefully on a yoga mat in the front of the room, facing the spaces where we would all sit. Her long, wild, and wispy hair was dancing about her shoulders, her lively eyes were bright, and her strong, gentle presence was deeply calming.

We chose colorful cushions from the assortment along the wall and settled onto the beautiful, original, wooden floors with big, warm blankets at the ready beside us. The floor was worn with the footsteps of many eager hearts who had been here before us and its golden-brown hue reminded me of the floors in my childhood home. The environment felt inviting and warm.

Nobody broke the silence.

The mystique of the session hung in the air.

Our retreat center was remote in an intentionally off-the-grid location. The use of technology and screens was discouraged, TVs were nonexistent on the property, and they shut off the internet after sunset. There was no big projector screen in our gathering space. So, when our leader told us that we were going to start with a video, we were all a bit surprised.

She opened up a small, black laptop and put it on the ground beside her.

She let the anticipation in the room settle as she led us through a few deep breaths. She didn't offer much of a preamble but told us to pay close attention to what we were going to see.

We all abandoned our cushions and huddled close to the small screen. Our attention was focused intently on it.

The video started like an old-time movie as the black screen faded to pure white.

Five or six black lines, and a handful of black dots appeared. They configured themselves into several different shapes, moving from place to place or staying in a fixed location for a while.

Some of them moved fast, others slowly.

Some stayed in one quadrant of the screen, others wandered about.

At one point, four of the lines came together to make a large square box centered in the middle of the frame. One of the dots was inside of the box. Another dot was outside of the box. The outside dot was tapping the outside of the box quickly and repeatedly. The dot inside of the box was bouncing rapidly, seemingly in response.

One of the lines, at the top of the box, tilted, making a little slanted opening, a doorway, an entry of sorts.

There were no words.

There was no music, no sound of any kind.

Just the lines and dots moving and shifting with our hungry eyes riveted to their activities.

The outside dot bounced its way up the side of the box and eventually got into the box through the opening at the top. The inside dot moved around. They didn't intersect.

The lines drifted apart, the box disassembled, the dots faded and the video concluded.

There was intent silence.

Even the room itself was hushed and the early night outside was still, under a big, expansive, starry sky.

Our leader asked us what we had seen.

Some people focused on the dots and lines involved in the box formation, as I had; others in the group observed more closely the lines and dots not involved in the box compilation. For some participants, the scene seemed to be a dance, for others a fight. Some saw a full story while others saw several mini stories or disjointed scenes.

A few of the ladies thought it was an uplifting story of one dot seeking something lost, others, me included, concluded something radically different. We saw something sinister and adversarial happening between the inside and outside dot, something threatening and ill-intentioned.

Narrative after narrative emerged.

There was overlap in some of them, but no two were exactly the same and many were wildly different from each other.

Several of us had expected that there would be a correct interpretation of the video and I was not alone in feeling frustrated when we continued to ask what the right answer was and our leader continued to tell us that it was just dots and lines, lines and dots.

There was no intrinsic meaning, no set narrative.

I wanted to be right about the meaning and I stewed about it for nearly half the session. When I could finally let go of my expectation of correct and incorrect interpretations, I got more than the being-on-the-good-side approval I had been seeking.

I got insight.

You see, she wasn't focused on what the correct or incorrect interpretation of those dots and lines were. She was focused on what we did with our observation of them. Each and every one of us crafted a story. We saw dots and lines, and connected them into a meaningful narrative of some nature.

I myself was so attached to my interpretation of the assemblage and disassemblage of those moving shapes that I fumed for nearly an hour over not getting the gratification of having gotten it right.

And it made her point so much more poignant when I could finally be receptive to it.

"Your stories can empower or disempower you. And you have the power to choose," she said.

She was giving us a visceral experience of how vital narrative, story, is to our human experience. We crave a narrative, and we make meaning about everything around us and within us.

"Your stories can empower or disempower you. And you have the power to choose," she repeated.

She said those phrases over and over throughout the course of the evening.

The first time she said them, I found them interesting; the next time I found them deeply intriguing and, by the third time, they had rooted in my mind and, even more importantly, in my heart.

Our stories can power or disempower us.

And we have the power to choose.

As self-reflective beings, humans can see ourselves and those around us.

We observe events, objects and people, and those observations are filtered into our visual right brain, the seat of awareness, recognition, and emotion. Our verbal left brain, the control center for reading, writing, and logic, requires a narrative, a story to make sense of what our visual right brain observes, to make it comprehensively useful to us.

So story, narrative, isn't just a nice-to-have or a vague desire within us: it is a core necessity, an essential, internal, communication modality, a mechanism through which we are able to glean information about how the world works and how we function within it.

No matter what the pieces are and how much they are or are not related, humans crave a narrative to hold the pieces together. And story is composed of heroes and villains, of tests and trials, of conclusions and morals.

In a word, meaning.

When we perceive a meaning, when we draw a conclusion, when we internalize a belief, we are hardwired to seek evidence to confirm what we hold true, what we know, what we believe. To find that evidence, we align our awareness to the pieces around us—the people, places, circumstances, situations, things—that fit within the paradigm of what we are looking to confirm.

We zero in on what confirms, and we delete, distort and generalize almost everything else.

It takes effort to exit from a narrative, to redirect our focus to facts that support a *new* narrative.

The adage that old habits die hard is true because each one of us has developed neural pathways—habit of selection, of thought and of interpretation—and when we shift our narrative, we have to override old habits of thought, while cultivating new ones.

It is easy to drift into a disempowering narrative, to accidentally live in the genre of tragedy—like I did in my relationship with Paul—but we will rarely shift our narrative towards empowerment without a conscious and concentrated effort to do so. In order to make the shift, we first have to know, to understand, and to accept where we are.

And sometimes that can be harder than it seems.

Early on in my intense healing journey, I had decided to work with a tantra instructor, Elsbeth. She and I belonged to the same organization. As business owners, we had both decided to work with a mentor for a year to help us grow our businesses. We were attending our first big event as part of that organization. It was a fairly large group and many of us, probably 150 or so people, had gathered together for an inspiring few days of workshops.

Throughout the week, Elsbeth and I had only intersected in passing. Her specialty was so unique that I had taken notice of her, but I had dismissed what she did out of hand as inapplicable to me.

However, on the last night of the event, we both ended up catching a ride in the same minivan heading back from dinner to the resort. I was tired and, since I had really invited myself to tag along in their vehicle, I was sitting by myself in the back row. She and one of our male peers were in the first row of the van behind the driver.

He was asking her about how she got into tantra. We were the only three passengers, so I couldn't help but overhear the story she shared. I knew nothing about tantra at the time and, like most people, associated it with long, passionate lovemaking. I don't remember all the specifics of her story, but a few things struck me. First off, she didn't talk about sex at all. There was nothing bawdy about her demeanor or explicit in the least. In fact, there was something almost austere about her and yet she talked with a sense of warmth and heart that caught me off guard.

I don't know why, but I had expected something less refined.

It wasn't because of her. She was the picture of elegance. Tall, slim, with short blonde hair and pale white skin that verged on translucent. Her spirit was lively and vital and she wore her age beautifully. The combination made her look fresh and youthful and wise.

And then, she told her story with a level of comfort and ease that struck me.

She talked about how she had been in a long-term relationship with a married man—a relationship that had made her feel less and less good and that brought her to the brink of suicide. She talked about having been sexually abused in her younger years and how she sought safety in such a limited and limiting relationship.

I listened more and more attentively.

She said that she had been invited to a tantra retreat by a friend who really wanted to help her find the courage to walk away from the man who would never be hers. She kept going back to him and couldn't seem to find a way to stop herself. She hadn't known what she was getting into with the retreat but felt like she should go, so she did, almost spontaneously.

She was so surprised at what she found.

She found healing there.

She found a new respect for herself, her body, the sacredness of her sexuality. She found a way to confront her story with gentleness but firmness too. And all of it without shame or fear or hiding. There was no big, grave, moral imperative trying to force her one way or another, there was only love. Love of self. Respect of self. Honoring of self.

For the first time in her life, she saw herself, her body, her sexuality, as something truly beautiful and to be honored.

It was like nothing she had ever experienced before and it gave her a courage that she had never had. The week after the retreat, she walked away from her lover and never looked back.

Her life was transformed.

From there, she became a student, a practitioner, and then eventually a teacher of tantra.

By the end of the bus ride, I knew I had to speak to her. Her story resonated with pieces of mine and if tantra had been so transformative for her, perhaps it could be a vehicle for the healing I was looking for too.

They were still chatting when the van parked and I lingered outside of the van, waiting to see if I could catch a word with her.

I know better than to assume that these moments, these sorts of chance meetings are happenstance or coincidence.

They are not.

They are moments of divine intervention—moments when we are helped along our journey if only we are willing to overcome the discomfort, to endure the awkwardness, to embrace the vulnerability, and to act. Too often the window of opportunity opens, and it passes before we find the courage to step out of our comfort zone and see what might be there for us.

I certainly didn't want to miss this chance.

There is an adage that when the student is ready, the teacher appears. And I wanted to see if maybe, just maybe, I was ready.

So as soon as she stepped out of the van, I introduced myself, exchanged contact details with her and, within a week or two, we had our first official consultation.

I came to her because I felt that sexual trauma from my early twenties was to blame for my consistent pursuit by unavailable men. It has been going on, off and on, for nearly two decades and, in my twenties I would joke that if there were one hundred single men in a room and only one married man, the only one who would approach me would be the married one. It was so strange. It was as though good, emotionally healthy, available men didn't even see me, but the ones who were unavailable were drawn to me like a moth to a flame.

And they weren't always married or otherwise committed. The flavors of unavailability were quite varied: drug addiction, alcoholism, workaholism, emotional unavailability—all of it.

And I was far from perfect. I had gotten involved with some of them. For those who were committed elsewhere, I knew it was wrong. I didn't really want to be doing it, but I would. It was a source of shame and confusion for me, and I found myself on a constant pilgrimage to and from the confessional week after week. Adultery went against everything I believed in and yet, there I was.

When I started talking with Elsbeth, I hadn't pursued any relationships or connections with married men in many years, but being newly single, I was afraid it would happen again. In fact, I was terrified that it would.

I was like a magnet for them, and I did not want to be.

I had tried prayer.

I had tried will power.

That had not been enough in the past, and I had no reason to believe it would be enough now.

I needed something more.

I needed to fix this at its root and, since I was in the early stages of my quest to mend my woundedness after my relationship with Paul, I felt this was the right time to do it.

I told Elsbeth my full history on that first call and she felt that she would be able to help me. They offered lots of different retreats and workshops at her facility in Chicago, but she recommended a private retreat just for me so that we could make the progress I craved.

I accepted the invitation.

One complicating factor to making that yes work was caring for my son while I would be gone.

We were still living with my mom and dad outside of Detroit and mom would watch Noah for me every day while I worked, but I didn't want to burden her too much by taking non-work days away when Noah wasn't with his Dad. And this private retreat would be over one of my weekends, so I needed to ask for her help to watch my son.

The other complicating factor was that my parents are intensely Catholic. They raised us all in the most traditional practice of the faith and expected us to live by its principles. I was and am Catholic too, but, as you just discovered, I hadn't always been so good about the no-sex-outside-of-marriage part. I had a son, so of course she knew that, but I was still hesitant to tell her the full truth of why I was going and what type of retreat it would be. I thought she would judge me for seeking the help of a Tantra instructor and that she might feel it wasn't within the scope of our faith.

I couldn't have been more wrong.

She knew I needed this healing. She knew I was wounded. I had told her bits and pieces of my history before and she was wise enough to read between the lines to fill in the rest. She didn't judge me. She had long prayed for me to find my way out of it and now, as I was reaching out for healing, she supported me fully. She encouraged me to go and do what I needed to do and told me she would do all that she could to help me.

She was proud of me.

She knew it wasn't easy to acknowledge that I needed this support and that it wasn't easy to let my walls down enough to get it.

I was so touched.

I felt so deeply loved and so warmly supported that I knew I had made the right decision.

I was peaceful about it.

I didn't know exactly what to expect for the two and a half days I was going to spend at the retreat center. I knew that there would be no nudity of any kind whatsoever and that this wasn't about physicality. Other than that, I was going on faith.

I had assumed that we would jump right into the sexual side of things and that we would look at what had triggered my promiscuity, but we didn't do that.

We started with me.

We started with self-love.

We started with me being willing to love myself. Not in the conditional or the remote way that I had done in the past, but in an intimate way, from the inside out. Loving who I was at the core, loving my body, loving where I was in my life exactly at that moment regardless of the squirrely path I may have taken to get there.

And she taught me meditation and breathing techniques to help me embody what I had learned in very real and practical ways.

I was deeply moved. Tears flowed freely.

That was the first half of day one.

She opened my eyes to myself so gently, so respectfully, so lovingly. I had never felt as accepting of myself, so appreciative of the vessel of my body, so aware of my heart.

After lunch, we settled in for what would be one of our longer sessions. It was a conversation, blended with a therapy session, wrapped up with a waking meditation of sorts. We started by grounding ourselves with some really beautiful breathwork and then we jumped into the discussion of my can't-stop-attracting-married-men thing. She asked me if that was something I wanted to address with her today.

"Of course! That's one of the big reasons I'm here."

"Great. So, why do you think that keeps happening?"

"Well, it's safe. There is no obligation on me. They are committed elsewhere, so there are no expectations or pressure. It's a partial relationship. We can date and enjoy each other and have fun, but then they go home and that's it. It had always felt easy in a way. But I'm not the one pursuing them, they are the ones pursuing me. Sometimes I didn't even know they were married until we had been dating for a few weeks. I don't really know what it is. It's like I have a neon sign, 'unavailable men only', floating above my head."

"Well, while those things may certainly be valid, I don't think that's really the reason."

I suggested that maybe it stemmed from a trauma that had happened when I was twenty. She found even that unlikely.

She told me that when we are stuck in a pattern of behavior that we don't consciously want, there is an underlying belief driving us and it is usually something that got implanted very early on in our lives. We have to go back to those young years and find out what it is, because if we don't find that belief and let it go, it's very unlikely that the behavior will change.

I had had a very happy childhood and didn't feel like there was anything that could have made me drive towards this behavior, so I was skeptical, but I sat there, on my meditation cushion, looking at her and listening. I was doing my best to suspend my skepticism for the moment. I had paid a lot of money and had shuffled a ton of things in my schedule to be here, and I wanted to embrace her work fully.

"Who was your first love?"

"My dad!" I responded without the least glimmer of hesitation.

"Ok. So, tell me about that. Tell me about him."

I told her how my dad had always been my hero. He was my person. He always got me and loved me unconditionally. Our relationship was easy.

I told her how he had overcome his struggle with alcoholism nearly twenty-five years earlier, but when I was a little girl, he had been a very severe alcoholic. He wasn't a mean or angry drunk, just an absent one. I didn't remember him drinking much at home—maybe a beer here or there in the hot summer months—but I did know that he drank a lot, so I deduced that what I saw as a kid as long working hours were probably long drinking hours with his buddies.

"So, he was unavailable?"

Writing it now, it seems so clear and so ridiculously obvious, but until that very moment, I had never seen it before.

It was right there in front of me, but I had never put two and two together.

I had been looking down and sort of wandering my eyes around the room as I had been speaking, making intermittent eye contact with Elsbeth. She had been gazing at me attentively, listening to every word I was saying.

The second she asked that question, my eyes snapped to hers. The rush of surprise and realization and shock flashed through my whole body and I flushed all over. I was hot and cold at the same time. My eyes were wide, my face and body frozen still.

She maintained eye contact.

Her face was neutral, her eyes gentle. She radiated a supporting presence.

The room was still and silent.

"He was unavailable." She said it again, but in a reassuring and compassionate tone this time, not a question.

"He was." I answered in a sort of disbelieving but relieved tone of voice.

I crinkled up my forehead and my nose and just looked at her. I was recovering from the shock of it while she went on to explain what happened in my subconscious mind as a child.

She told me that when I was really little, and the man I loved the most in the whole wide world was constantly unavailable to me, I drew a conclusion that love and unavailability were joined like two links in a big metal chain. One did not exist without the other.

They were inseparable.

She told me that little Madeleine was still there in my subconscious mind, holding onto the belief she crafted that when a person loves you, they are not available to you. And that belief was running the show without me even knowing it. It was so deeply part of my perception of how the world worked that it came out as attracting that reality.

She said that we all do this. As children, we observe people and events around us and make conclusions about how the world works. It's how we are designed as human beings. And when what we have been holding onto is no longer serving us, it is our responsibility, as adults, to figure out what it is exactly and then to work to change it.

I told her how I had been trying to change it from the outside and how much I tried to muscle through with will power. I talked to her about not wanting to be doing the wrong thing and she said something fascinating to me.

Good and bad, right and wrong, are beginner strategies.

They are what you need to get started, but when your conscience has been formed, and you are at this stage of your emotional, intellectual, psychological development, you will not find those paradigms as compelling. And she suggested that I look at my choices in quite another way.

She had me go from my comfortably seated position to a reclining position so that my body could rest while my mind processed what I had just discovered, and we took the discovery deeper.

She had me do a sort of meditation that looked something like this:

Fast-forward yourself a few years from now and look around at where you are. Imagine that you are exactly where you want to be. What does it look like? Where are you? What sort of woman have you become?

As I was thinking about that and imagining it in my mind, she told me that we cannot become something if we do not walk in its direction.

I knew that to be true. My dad had always told me that a tree falls as it leans and I watched that play out in business and in life many times over.

After she confirmed that I was tracking with her, she offered me a new idea. She posited that instead of the good/bad, right/wrong paradigm that I was used to considering, I should consider if the action I'm thinking of taking, the thing that I am doing or thinking of doing, is congruent or incongruent with the person I want to be, the person I'm becoming.

Every choice shapes us.

Every choice becomes part of our narrative, weaving our story.

When we think of things in the context of congruence, the weight of the must, the feeling of being forced, the should and should-nots shift. Obligation transforms into desire. Desire pulls us forward and we walk more freely.

When we know who we want to become and we are consistently doing the opposite or something that is not pointing us in that direction, we can be fairly certain that there is deep belief underpinning those actions that needs to be observed and relinquished.

My body was already relaxed at this point, and it was as though the weight of all of those decisions, the shame of them, lifted from me and just evaporated. I knew that asking myself if my decisions were aligned or misaligned, congruent or incongruent, with the woman I wanted to be and to become, would lead me down the path I truly wanted to be on without all of the emotional turmoil.

It was freeing.

I almost felt like I was floating.

And then she asked me if I wanted to let go of my belief that when a person loves you, they are not available to you.

Of course I did.

She had me imagine that I was holding a big, heavy, metal chain and, in my imagination, she had me grip the part that represented Love and the part that represented Unavailability and just pull those two links apart.

It was easy. They slipped apart like butter.

The metal looked shiny and the links were huge—almost like big, plastic, chrome-covered toys. They weren't heavy in my hands but my mind knew they had heft.

And then she had me pile up the whole chain—now in two separate pieces—and hold it with both hands and hurl it with all the strength I could muster over the city of Chicago, all the way into Lake Michigan. I chucked it hard and I watched it twist and turn as it soared over the skyscrapers and landed with an impressive splash into the cold deep water.

The waves rippled over the surface.

She had me draw the attention of my inner eye to the chain as it sank all the way to the bottom. Down, down, down. Past where the sunlight lit the water to the deepest part of the lake where it would stay forever, unlinked, removed from me, put to rest. Gone.

That was it.

All of those years of angst and of suffering and of feeling mystified and mortified by my own bad decisions were behind me.

A pair of golden scissors had cut the thread.

I was no longer bound.

And never again has an unavailable man—a truly unavailable man—tried to pursue me in any serious way.

Never again has the idea of a partial relationship felt good or inviting or safe.

I had always wanted more than what I would sometimes settle for and, free of the bondage of that childhood belief, I have walked joyfully in the direction of the woman I am, the woman I want to be, the woman I am becoming.

When big shifts happen, it can be hard to adapt to our new selves and our new narrative. Things that are new can feel foreign. When our vision of ourselves, our perspective, is outdated, it is time to get a new snapshot of who and where we are.

I call this needing a new polaroid.

It's a concept I got from the CEO, Michael, who mentored me throughout my corporate career. Michael was a brilliant business-man and he knew how to play the game masterfully. It was a quality I always admired.

He was the leader of the North American division of a billion-dol-lar, multinational organization and the corporate leaders would come to our New Jersey facility from France a couple of times a year. He would prepare fastidiously every time, but for one particular visit I thought he was going overboard.

He was having the windows washed, inside and out, the side-walks power washed, carpet tiles and light bulbs replaced, draperies that had been ready for months finally hung. And, one afternoon, as we were coming down the stairs together, I spotted a painter doing touch-ups. I had been wondering why he was going all out this time and I couldn't help but ask him about it.

"So, Michael, what's going on with all of the preparations? It seems like we are doing way more than we ever have before. It's the same group that came last year, right? Why are we going nuts?"

He looked at me with an indulgent smile. He understood that, although my questions were a little critical, I truly wanted to under-stand his motives.

"Well, we are going to be making some seriously large asks of the parent company this year. We are going to present an ambitious five-year budget and it's going to take some funding and really essential support. We've been growing steadily every year, but now we are going to pour some gas on the fire.

"While they are here," he continued to explain, "they are going to be taking one long, extended picture of who we are. In the eyes of their mind, they are going to see and notice everything and are going to put it into that picture. When they leave, they will tuck that polaroid into the breast pocket of their blazer. Every time we ask for something, every time we request an improvement to a product, additional headcount, marketing support, every time we ask for more or better from them, they are going to take out that picture and look at it good and hard.

"If we have any chance of success, that picture has to be of us at our very best.

"It might feel like we are going over the top, but we have to show our building, our facility, our team at its peak. It's like getting dressed up to go on a nice date. You take the time and effort to be at your best. It's not the way you might look on a lazy Sunday morning and that's ok.

"We need to be at our best.

"If they don't take a good polaroid, we may not ever get to where we want to grow."

I listened intently.

I hadn't ever considered that people take a polaroid of us—of us as an organization and of us an individual—and that the one the big bosses had was too outdated to support us, practically, so we needed to create the conditions for a dramatically updated picture.

It was an absolute necessity.

People judge the book by the cover, and for individuals, as much as for organizations, the cover shouldn't be an entirely static image.

Change is happening all the time; growth is happening when we allow it and we need to be aware of the polaroid we're holding onto.

This is not only true for businesses, but it is also—and sometimes even more dramatically—true for ourselves.

When big changes happen to our bodies, if we gain or lose a dramatic amount of weight for example, our faces change. We are still identifiable, but we truly look different.

As go our external bodies, so too, our inner selves. When we are on a growth trajectory, when we have a huge shift in how we see or approach the world around us, we may look different, on the inside, even to ourselves.

When we judge ourselves by the wrong standard, when we are looking at a polaroid that was handed to us, maybe taken with the wrong lens, we might feel smaller, dimmer, less incredible than we truly are. And if our polaroid is old and outdated, we may underestimate what we are capable of, we may unintentionally limit our own potential, we may stay stuck when opportunity opens up in front of us.

You have to be brave in order to take the polaroid that other people took of you —maybe from an unflattering vantagepoint—or that you took of yourself long ago, and you set it aside.

Replace it.

Whether it's the image of yourself, or the image of how you thought your life, your career, your family, your business would be, let it go. Set it aside if it's not empowering you to step forward into all that you are, all that you can be, and take a new picture.

And we certainly can.

We have the power, the responsibility, to update our polaroid when we realize that it's no longer an accurate description of who we are on the inside, of where we are in our own narrative, and of how we want to proceed forward.

Making decisions in the context of congruence or incongruence forces me to know who I am, know who I want to become, and not only to act accordingly but also to see myself accordingly.

Whether we are doing it on purpose or not, we are always weaving our narrative. And it is so liberating to do it intentionally, congruently, peacefully, with a current and accurate picture of who you truly are.

It's incredible to experience the new horizons that open when you're living in an empowering narrative with a fresh new polaroid.

CREATING YOUR NARRATIVE

Every time I work with a new client, I do a process with them that I call The Champagne Process. It's a simple but powerful visualization that allows the deeper desires of the heart to speak. I've used it for so many things: board retreats, private coaching, strategic planning, fundamental values work. It's a versatile resource that I've used for a long time and it's one that I do, personally, every year for myself.

And I want to share it with you. It's very simple. You are going to love it!

Bring a piece of paper and something to write with and then go to a place that is calm and quiet. Sit comfortably. Breathe deeply. Calm your mind. Settle your inner chatter. Still your body.

Take a few deep breaths.

Now imagine that you are somewhere absolutely beautiful, safe, uplifting—a place that you truly enjoy. It is one year from now and you are there with someone who loves, supports and believes in you unconditionally. I call them your cheerleader. They can be here with you on earth or already passed on. Just imagine that person there with you.

See the scene in detail in the eye of your mind. Look around yourself. Take a few deep breaths. Smile. Relax.

Suspend all disbelief for a moment and assume that you have done all you set out to do in this past year. Look back over the year and, as if giving a heartfelt toast that isn't cute or contrived, tell your person what you are toasting. What made you proud? What have you done or accomplished?

Don't edit yourself. Let the joy flow out as it will. Speak it to them in your mind or aloud and then write it out.

Once it's written, read what you put on your paper a couple times. Let it seep into your heart.

Then read it through again and underline the most meaningful phrases.

Give it a title if you can.

Let this serve as your intention statement for the year.

It doesn't have to be hard or complicated or take a long time to do. Let it be easy. Let it flow. Your heart knows what you most deeply desire. Trust it.

Take things deeper at:
www.madeleinemacrae.com/gifts

♡ Madeleine

CHAPTER 5

THE NUDGE

"Let him be rich and weary, that at least,
If goodness lead him not, yet weariness
May toss him to my breast."

— THE PULLEY, GEORGE HERBERT

THE SOCKS.

T HERE THEY WERE AGAIN. Staring at me from the middle of the living room floor like two live creatures taunting me.

That was it! I had had enough. I just couldn't take it for one more second.

Something had to change.

Years ago, my son and I had a live-in nanny staying with us in our home, let's call her Evelyn. She was a lovely person and helped our family tremendously during a time when I was, like many other moments in my life, in transition.

She was the daughter of a dear friend of our family. I had actually been her babysitter when I was younger and she was a tiny girl, so there was something satisfyingly synchronistic about her now living with my little family, taking care of my son. I knew her well. She was a good girl. Reliable. Trustworthy. Patient. Kind. Devout. Prayerful. All the things you would want in someone responsible for caring for your child, responsible for helping you raise him. She was a good example not only to my son, but to me too. She was just the right person to help my sweet little boy navigate emerging moments in his young life. Though they were both undiagnosed at the time, we later discovered that she, like my son, had Autism Spectrum Disorder and so, as an adult, she brought techniques and coping mechanisms to the table for him—and for me—that I would never have imagined to use.

She was a great gift to us.

And she did more for me than she will ever know.

But Evelyn was messy. Not the tie-back-your-hair-into-a-cute-little-messy-bun sort of messy, the make-a-mess-and-don't-even-notice sort of messy. The leave-your-socks-in-the-living-room-and-your-unfinished-crafts-on-the-dining-room-table sort of messy. In some ways she was organized and thorough and in other ways, not. It drove me crazy. My home is my sanctuary. It's my place of refuge from the big decisions I need to make, from the external turmoil around me. It is where I refuel and recharge so that I can go back out there and run at full tilt.

In my home I crave peace. One of the things that has been consistent for me throughout my life is that, in order for an environment to be restful and peaceful, it needs to be neat, clean, and uncluttered. In my earlier years, prior to having a child, I kept my home hotel-clean at all times and, to this day, that's my ideal level of organization and cleanliness. True, it's a high bar, but for me it's a fundamental need.

Visual clutter and messiness don't allow me to attain the level of unplug and rest that my high-test life requires me to have during my downtime.

Evelyn knew this before she moved in with us. When I mentioned that I was looking for a nanny and she offered to relocate across the county for the position, we had a very open, honest conversation about cleanliness and the standard I would expect if she lived with me. While Noah and I lived in Michigan, prior to our relocation to Phoenix, Evelyn had babysat for us now and then. She always made great food and took excellent care of my son, but she would leave a mess behind her. It was fine for an occasional babysitter, but it would not be fine while she was living with us.

So we came to an agreement and Evelyn took a six-month position as our live-in nanny. I needed her because I was traveling to a client-site weekly and wanted someone with her incredible traits and good character to stay overnight with my little man. Because I was gone for a few days at a time each week, the relative tidiness of the house wasn't too much of a big deal.

But, when that assignment ended and I was back at home full time, it started to wear on me.

I didn't mind cleaning up after my son, but cleaning up after someone I was paying to make my life easier and better didn't sit well with me.

We talked about it quite a few times. Daily, it felt like to me.

Some days it would be the socks or a craft, other days it would be books or papers, and yet other days it would be unfinished chores like doing all the dishes except a spoon, a plate, and a cookie sheet—all of which sat on the counter or in the sink when the rest of the dishes were done.

It drove me nuts.

Yes, it was a small thing, but I struggled with it.

That fateful day when I came home from an event in the early evening and was greeted by those darn socks in the middle of the living room was a day on which I knew I needed to make an important decision. Evelyn's six-month contract was nearly complete, and I needed to go forward for another six or call it quits. I felt like it was time to end the arrangement. But what she did for us was so important and so helpful that I felt torn. I was caught between hating the ongoing frustration of the messiness and loving all the rest—and there was so very much to love.

I was stuck, so I decided to get a totally unbiased, outside opinion.

I asked a few of the people I loved and trusted for recommendations for a great local therapist. The same name kept popping up with everyone I asked. I had heard of her before. My sister had seen her. I knew her to be a no-nonsense straight-talker. Someone who would dish out the truth to you even if it wasn't easy to hear or popular to say. Just what I needed, I thought to myself! She will know what I should do!

So, I went to her website to grab an appointment. Her session slots were only thirty minutes, and you could only sign up for one at a time. No recurring options were available. It annoyed me that I couldn't get more time with her, but I figured that we would do as much as we could in the short session, and I pushed confirm.

I was excited about going to therapy again. I had gone many times throughout my life to unlock trauma's hold on me, to up-level my game, and even to tune things up internally when I wasn't feeling like myself. This time felt like a mix between an up-level and a tune-up.

That question I had been obsessing over about Evelyn really needed to be resolved and I knew I needed support to come to a resolution that would honor her contribution and support both of our needs.

When the day arrived, I was running late.

I only had thirty minutes with my therapist, and I felt the pressing sense of lost time bearing down on me as I rushed around the court-yard looking for the door to her suite. With each passing second, I was getting more and more perturbed. And, in those few frantic moments I realized that I was holding it together on the outside, but on the inside, the feeling of anxiety and stress that was mounting was so common that it almost felt normal to me. In that hurried search, I started to become vaguely aware that things were more off for me than I had realized before. I'm typically quick with a smile and a silver lining interpretation of even the most difficult circumstances but these days I struggled to find my happy, and a pair of socks on the living room floor, a few errant dishes in the sink, and this tardy start to an important meeting were putting me into a tailspin.

I was slipping into depression, and I didn't like it.

I had to fix the sock issue; that would resolve things, I knew it!

I could never have guessed that that appointment would change my life forever.

When I arrived and settled into her small and somewhat cramped office, we didn't waste much time on paperwork or perfunctory questions. I gave her a tiny bit of background: solo Mom, son's dad isn't a participant and lives in NYC. Business owner, work requires some travel, live-in nanny who is great but has some issues that consistently irritate me. The synopsis I gave didn't have much more meat on the bone than that run-down did and we jumped right in.

We talked about my home and how I live. We discussed my need for rest and how cleanliness and organization are conditions needed for me to find repose. We talked about the physical spaces within the house and how none of the spaces, aside from my own bedroom, were just for me. In discussing it, I realized that I needed space. A genuine space of my own, outside of my room, where it was just for me and was always mine. I needed a boundary within my living space so I could have a consistent refuge. I had vaguely recognized these things about myself before this conversation, but I saw them now in full relief. It was striking and liberating.

Giving voice to something important about yourself to yourself and to another person provides freedom that's hard to achieve in any other way.

The session was going great.

Five minutes in and already I was having genuine insights.

And then we started to talk more about the issues with Evelyn. I went on a little diatribe about the messiness and the constant conversations about it. I talked about how I had converted one of our linen closets into a "Evelyn overflow" space where I would put all the things that were left in common areas. I gave her a few dishes and socks examples and I concluded my tirade with the strong assertion, "It's just not working."

"It is working," my therapist stated plainly.

"Umm... no it's not. I just told you that I have to argue with her about this all the time. It's not working."

"It is working," she insisted again.

I started to get annoyed and said, "But I'm having to correct her all the time about this. I'm frustrated and the feeling in the house is tense. How is that working?"

"It's working for her."

"But I'm literally reprimanding her daily."

"And it's working for her."

I was dumbfounded. How could our session have gotten off track so fast? It seemed like we were having a total failure to communicate. I was listing all the ways in which the situation was not working. I was telling her how annoying and frustrating and unnecessarily repetitive all of this was, and she was baldly telling me that this situation was working.

I was about to object again and explain again why it was not working when she jumped in.

"Look," she said, "when someone does something more than twice, it is working for them."

Wow.

That was intense.

She looked me in the eye and repeated herself: "When someone does something more than twice, it is working for them."

She could see that I wasn't ready to be so easily swayed so she told me a shocking story about a little boy whose parents had brought him to her because his behavior was out of control. She told me that the mom, dad, and little boy all came to the session. The parents told her that every day when his dad would come home from work the little boy would go berserk. He would be disruptive and would engage in every forbidden behavior. He would hit his siblings, throw things, get loud, act unruly, damage the home, destroy toys. They had tried everything, and nothing was working.

It was a super stressful and destructive cycle that they didn't know how to break.

The parents were doing all the talking. They were explaining a particularly bad day that had just happened and my therapist interrupted them. She said she wanted to ask the boy to describe what was happening.

His story was quite different.

His story was that he would wait with a lot of joyful expectation for his dad to come home. He loved his dad and was always excited to see him. His dad would arrive home and would speak to his mom. He didn't like that. He wanted to speak to his dad. So he would get loud and do stuff until his dad stopped talking to his mom and talked to him. And then his dad would go back to speaking to his mom again, but he still wanted to talk to him, so he would do more stuff. He was doing it on purpose. He said that the night they were talking about, nothing was working so he kept going and going and going until finally he said, with delight on his face, "I got me my whooping."

My eyes nearly jumped out of my head.

She calmly explained that he was craving more than just conversation and attention. What he was really craving was correction. And he was getting it in the only way he knew how.

This ugly cycle was filling his emotional needs.

Was it good for him? No. Was it excellent parenting? Again, no. But it was working for the boy. It was meeting his emotional needs, so he continued.

Evelyn, she told me, is no different.

She explained that the cycle I was in with Evelyn was working for her. She was getting her emotional needs met. She was alone, far from family, with only a few friends and a lot of responsibilities in my home. Maybe she was craving attention or connection. Maybe she wanted to test a boundary or develop more of a friendship. Maybe it was something else entirely. Guessing the why was pure speculation without Evelyn in the room, but the point was clear.

Crystal clear.

No matter the reason, this was working.

It was working for Evelyn.

This cycle we were in was filling her emotional needs.

My therapist said to me one last time, "If a person does something more than twice, it's working for them."

I leaned back in my seat and said, half to myself, "It is working for her."

What an insight!

I had never considered that the reason it was hard to break this cycle was that I was trying to fix something that wasn't broken. It was working effectively on the other side of the relationship. There was not, of course, a conscious unwillingness on her side to change this pattern, but a subconscious emotional need was being so well met that we just couldn't work our way around it.

We spent a little time talking about the now-what of it all. Our arrangement had served Evelyn and me well but now I needed my physical and emotional space in a way I hadn't before my schedule had changed. We concluded that it was time to call it complete. We brainstormed an approach to the conversation that would preserve our relationship while making it clear that I would not be renewing the live-in nanny contract with her or with anyone else, for that matter.

I was at peace with the outcome.

It had been an intense conversation, but my therapist helped me find a pathway to a solution, with major insights provided. As our conversation concluded, she stepped over to her desk in the far corner of her room. She was checking to see if she had another patient coming in. She didn't and she offered the next half hour to me. Although the Evelyn topic had been resolved, there was a sense of unfinished business hanging in the air, and I took her up on her offer.

While I knew there was more broiling under the surface, I was resistant to discussing it because I didn't know how to express what I was feeling.

My therapist circled back to the hasty overview of my life and circumstances that I had given her at the beginning of our session, and, with a little prompting, I told her that I had been feeling trapped. I told her that I was stressed and starting to feel depressed. She looked me in the eye and said, "Well, Madeleine, depression is often a suppressed form of anger. What are you mad about?"

For the second time that day, I sat there stunned. And, just like the last time, I wasn't willing to accept her premise so easily. I responded to her that I wasn't angry about anything. But I could feel the anger welling up inside. I had to push it down so that it wouldn't come out in my words.

I was getting annoyed and upset. How dare she assume that I was angry. How presumptuous!

She heard the resistance in my voice as I continued to insist: "I'm not angry." And she stayed with it, stayed with me. She stood strongly in her assertion because she knew I couldn't bear to face it without her support.

I couldn't admit that I was raging mad.

Mad about something that was also one of the greatest joys of my life.

Mad about circumstances in my life that I was totally powerless to change.

Mad that I had been forced to set aside ambitions and dreams.

It was intolerable to me to be mad about it, so I denied it. I denied it to her, but even more importantly, I denied it to myself. The cause of my anger was so unacceptable to me, and I had hidden it so deeply inside that, sitting there on her couch, I couldn't even seem to admit that I was angry at all—even when it was seeping out in my tone and my body language and my fiery eyes.

But she stood in her strength, and I found the courage to tentatively explore some possibilities.

We talked more about my life, and my story started to piece together.

My heart was breaking because I love my son. My sweet little boy is the heartbeat outside of my body and yet, I was mad. I wasn't mad at him or at being a mom—I loved that. I was mad at having to do it on my own. I was mad that his dad abandoned his responsibilities wholesale and left me holding the whole parenting bag: physical, emotional, financial. The burden was heavy and to carry it I had been forced to make decisions that felt too hard to face.

When it came down to it, I was mad because I was a single, solo parent, and having to carry every piece of the parenting of my son limited my available time and energy to give to my work.

I was a solo mom and an ambitious entrepreneur.

I had always wanted to be a mom. From the time I was big enough to hold a baby I had known that being a mother was going to be part of my life in some way—having my son was a dream come true. It was a highly unexpected and unplanned pregnancy, but he was so wanted, so loved, so cherished. Even while desperately ill with morning sickness, I walked around on cloud nine when I was pregnant. I couldn't have been happier. He was all that I wanted. I hadn't ever dreamt of the white picket fence or the doting spouse, but I had dreamt of this: being a mom.

When I found out I was pregnant, my heart grew in a way that I never knew was possible.

And yet, here I was, sitting on the couch in this therapist's office, trying to find a way to talk about how angry I was over it.

It felt so disloyal and unloving to my son that I could hardly even choke out the words.

My two loves—contributing to the world through my work and raising my son—were raging an epic battle inwardly and I resented every part of it.

She let me pour the pieces out and then she told me that, whether I liked it or not, I was angry. Holding onto and suppressing that anger was not helping disappear the feelings.

Suppressing the anger was disappearing me.

That slow erosion of who I am—a joyful person full of joie de vivre—was showing up as depression and anxiety.

She told me I had to find a safe time and place to process the anger—to yell, to scream, to sob. I needed to cry it out, to let it out, to accept that was real.

She told me that, just as much as I needed physical space for myself within my home, I also needed to let my anger have some physical space, too.

She told me that I was blocking my anger because I couldn't allow myself to be mad at my son. She agreed with that. I could not and should not be mad at him. This wasn't his fault or his burden. And, truth be told, I wasn't mad at him at all. I loved him. He was everything to me. But I was angry over the circumstances I found myself in. And *that*, she told me, was something I was allowed to be mad about.

She gave me permission.

And even more than that, she told me I needed to let myself be red-hot, raging mad somewhere safe, sometime when my son wouldn't see me in my anger because he was too young to understand and too impressionable to be exposed to it.

That was a lot to take in.

She was right, of course, but it was a lot.

I left her office upset.

A whole flood of emotions that I'd bottled up for years started to bubble up and I could finally see them for what they were.

It took me a while to process what we had discussed, but it stayed with me, and I could feel the moment drawing nearer.

About a month later, after Evelyn had gone home for the holidays and I had my space to myself, I found the courage to allow the anger a safe space to come out. And, one night, after I had put my little man to bed and put some music on in the hallway so that he couldn't possibly hear me, I went into my room, closed and locked the door.

I knew it had to come out. It was overdue, but it wasn't familiar or comfortable.

At first I sort of went through the motions. I tried punching the pillows on my bed and then I started to think about everything and the anger welled up inside. It started to trickle out in hot burning tears rolling down my face. The flow of the tears acted like a release valve and, as they started to stream, everything else came pouring out too.

Now, the emotions were real.

I screamed into the pillows. I punched the mattress. I sobbed. I kicked. I shook with rage.

My whole body was involved and I let it all out—every single bit of lingering negative emotion.

I don't usually emote like that, but that night I did, and it felt almost euphoric.

When I had emptied it out completely and all my tears had dried, I felt a wave of calm come over me.

I craved some fresh air and I stepped into my backyard. The moonlight was so bright that I didn't even need to turn on a light.

I felt like I needed to write, so I grabbed my notebook and sat in the moonlight under the towering, swaying palm trees, and I wrote. My pen flew over the pages of my notebook, and I poured the struggle onto the page in the form of poetry. The anger that had festered inside was gone and I could see things in a way I hadn't before. I could recognize the struggle I had been in, and it showed up on the page in a type of poetry I hadn't ever written before.

I didn't see myself as a poet, and still don't, but the poem let the story take shape outside of me and gave me a place to express what I had been living. The story wasn't about my son or my nanny or my anger or my business at all. The story was about me. As it progressed on the page and I was in the middle of the transformational moment in the poem, the words seemed to get locked up. I couldn't see where it was going. I couldn't find the words or the way to bring it together, so I accepted that.

I let it be enough.

I set my pen aside and I went to bed tired, very tired, but incredibly happy and full of peace.

The poem was half written, and my story wasn't finished. I knew I wasn't going to let things go south, but I didn't know how they would get better.

Over the next few months, my happiness did return. My old, decisive self showed up in a way that she hadn't been able to for a long while and, every now and then, I would take my poem out and play with it a bit.

I did finally write an ending for the poem but it felt raw and unfinished.

And no matter how I would work and rework it, the second half of the poem just didn't flow. I tried every technique I knew. I changed the order of the words, replaced them with synonyms, broke up the lines. I inserted internal rhymes, disrupted the cadence, allowed imperfect rhymes and rhythms. Nothing seemed to work. All of my linguistic and poetic tricks felt too weak to hold up the turning point in the narrative and to make it all settle in cohesively. It seemed like the correct pieces were assembled but I couldn't seem to find a graceful way to bring them together.

The muse wasn't there to inspire me.

Or, more accurately, I wasn't there yet.

You see, this poem was and is an expression of my own inner journey, a journey of fear and of worry, of hope and of faith, of courage and of joy.

I was living it, but I wasn't on the other side of the story yet.

The year was 2020.

The pandemic trauma, the hurdles I had to pass, the way I had to step more and more fully into the woman I was, the woman I could be—mother, sister, mentor, businesswoman—as I worked through all that becoming, the poem slowly started to get unstuck. The phrases that wouldn't fit found their place, and as I became more and more willing to step into the light, to shine in my truest, brightest, most magnetic form, I found that the poem also came together.

It wasn't until after I had weathered one of the hardest losses, the biggest challenges of my life—the death of my Dad—that I found the words to complete the poem.

I was deep in grief, but I was no longer shoving my emotions down. I was accepting where I was, not with anger and resentment but with peacefulness. I was where I was supposed to be and I extended to my grief-stricken heart the kindness and patience that I would have shown to my dearest friend. I took the time I needed to grieve, and I was at peace even amid the tears.

And when I would pull out the journal where I was working on my poem, a few of the stubborn parts that felt raw, unfinished, imperfect would come together just a little bit more each time. It was a gradual process and, invariably, I would tweak the text and improve it and then set it aside still incomplete.

Until one day, late in the afternoon, when I took it out and read it aloud to myself. Lines that had, for so long, felt unfinished and imperfect, suddenly felt exactly right. I adjusted a phrase or two, added a little punctuation and I realized it was complete. Without me even realizing it, my poem had already found its ending. My journey was evolving and would continue to evolve, but this phase of playing small, hiding out from anger and other big unwelcome emotions was complete and I was ready to be, to do, and to have more!

No more could socks on the floor send me down a spiral.

The Skin
By Madeleine MacRae

My body has been growing, this skin no longer fits,
No matter how I move, or where, it tugs and tears and rips.

I've tried so long to keep it on;
    Without it I'd be bare,
I've stitched, I've sewn, I've stretched and pulled.
    I've patched it everywhere.

This skin, my skin, it has to go. It's worse than disrepair.
It's suffocating the beautiful self that's been growing under there.

I am afraid.
What if it hurts
To let this old skin go?

Far worse, she said,
To keep it on
And then to never know

The beauty, pow'r, strength and worth of th' exquisite creature;
She's waiting, trapped inside, waiting for you to meet her.

I feel afraid.
What if she's more, more than I can handle?
What if I make her goals and dreams
Come screeching to a standstill?

She fixed my gaze and raised her hand and bade me to come nearer.
As I approached, I could see, she was off'ring me a mirror.
"Look in," she said, "And tell the truth, are yours the eyes of a killer?"

My eyes looked scared but deep and kind
And, in the fading sunlight, golden.
She turned to me, grasped my hand;
I felt myself embolden.

"Cast fear aside and faithlessness and any shred of doubt.
Let it go. It is safe to let your new self out."

She spoke to me,
My inner voice, and suddenly I knew.
The time was now
To let it go. The words she said were true.

Instantly the spell was broke.
This was the final hour.
Those threads, once strong and binding,
Had finally lost their power.

I now was free, the old skin gone.
   And all within was peaceful.

CHAPTER 6

LIGHTNING ROD MOMENTS

"Don't let people pull you into their
storm. Pull them into your peace."

— PEMA CHODRON

**THE ROOM WAS BUBBLING WITH THE CHATTER OF
GOOD FRIENDS.**

I T WAS A COUPLE OF WEEKS shy of the end of my junior year in
college, and several of us girls had converged upon one of my
friend's places on the top floor of the dorms. The dorms were more
like full-fledged apartment suites than the standard college dorms
and the atmosphere was comfortable and inviting. I had found a
perfect spot on the plush carpeted floor, leaning against a couch,
and there were a few acquaintances of mine in the room.

One of my long-term, dear friends was hosting this little afternoon chat. She had already graduated and done several years in the
military but was back on campus, working at the library.

We were having a few drinks, sharing stories about life and eventually the conversation reverted to boys. I decided to share the story
of my first time with a man. I told an abridged version of my story
but, even with that, one of the girls looked me dead in the eyes and
said, "You know that's rape, right?"

I was taken aback.

You could have knocked me down with a feather.

I got hot and cold all over one right after another.

Embarrassment and anger were welling up inside of me, but I shoved it all down and suppressed my emotions. And engaged in a strictly academic conversation of what did and didn't constitute rape. I put myself firmly on the safe side of the line I had drawn in my own head, and I insisted I had not been raped. She held firm that I had been. It went on for what seemed like forever, and when it was clear that we were at an impasse, and that I was in no humor to be swayed, one of my other friends bailed me out by breaking into the conversation and changing the subject entirely.

What a relief.

I lingered for a few moments and then quietly got up and left the room.

I walked down the two flights of stairs back to my own floor in a daze. I had fought her on it, but the intensity of what I had just realized started to sink in more and more with each step. My stomach started to churn. My footsteps quickened so I could make it to my bathroom in time.

I burst into my room, ran to the toilet and barfed my brains out.

The wrenching feeling in the pit of my stomach quelled and I took a deep breath, straightened out my hair, brushed my teeth and went back upstairs to the conversation like nothing had happened.

But something had happened.

In one flash, my conscious mind and my subconscious mind reconciled the awful fact of what had happened nearly six months earlier. And I finally knew what had been wrong with me all those months. That one missing puzzle piece made the whole picture clear.

I had been raped.

I was traumatized. Deeply traumatized.

It was a devastating realization.

Well over a year earlier I had been accepted into the study abroad program that our tiny college offered. It was an incredible program offered in partnership with another, much larger, university from the States and was offered in conjunction with a doctoral study program based in Gaming, Austria.

Studying abroad had been one of my non-negotiables in selecting a school for my college studies and I had been looking forward to that semester for years.

And it did not disappoint.

The courses were interesting and challenging, but I hadn't come just for the study. I had come for the experience and the travel.

The handful of students from our college shared space—both classes and living space—with the doctoral program students. We occupied an incredibly gorgeous wing of an 800-year-old monastery nestled in the foothills of the Austrian Alps.

The walls were stone and the atmosphere felt reverent and welcoming.

It was early fall.

The views were breathtaking.

Frost would dance on the still-green grass; sheep would graze on the hill outside the windows at all hours of the day. Our voices would echo through the vaulted stone passageways.

The locals were friendly and accommodating.

It felt like we were living in a storybook. Idyllic. Wholesome. Delightful.

I was only a few months shy of my twenty-first birthday and spent long weekends exploring Europe. The Kartause—the official name of our incredibly cool Austrian campus—was less than a two-hour drive from Vienna, Austria and we could get to the city, to neighboring countries, and all over Austria quickly and easily by train. Our Fridays were free every other week and my friends and I spent long weekends traveling, exploring, enjoying the history and beauty of it all.

When we weren't out and about, the local pub at the end of a winding path through the woods or straight down the mountain on the main road was a frequent haunt for us as well as for the students of our American sister-school. Their program was at least ten times the size of ours, so we were only a small contingent of the Americans who frequented that pub.

That year, on Halloween, all of the various contingents of the campus were meeting at the pub for a costume party.

Now, I'm not much of a costume person even to this day, but at that phase of my life, I was hardly even comfortable in my own skin, much less in a costume. I was painfully aware of the awkward boarding-school-girl side of me when I knew I would be around cute guys. I had absolutely no idea how to flirt. Some of my friends might say that I still don't.

So, I was excited, but I was nervous too. There was one boy in particular that I had a huge crush on from our sister school. He was cute and popular and blonde and tall and probably didn't even know I existed. Still, I wanted to make a good impression on the off-chance he might, so I put in far more effort than I would have otherwise.

None of us had true costumes that year. I borrowed a green and brown sarong from one of my Latin American friends, a pair of Birkenstocks from another, and someone did my hair and makeup. The costume was complete. I was ready to have fun.

It was dusk and the forest was a bit cold and dark, so a group of my girlfriends and I walked down to the pub along the main road together.

Inside it was warm and cozy. The small building was buzzing with the chatter of friends gathering and smelled of freshly tapped beer. The big, burly gentleman behind the bar gave us warm, approving smiles as we walked in. We each got a huge glass stein of local beer and posted up at one of our favorite high-top tables along the back wall of the main room. People were mulling around, chatting, laughing, drinking.

The costumes were great. Rugby players, cheerleaders, and all manner of make-shift costumes plundered from the closets and suitcases of friends.

The cute boy I liked was absorbed in his friend group. We hardly made eye contact, but there was another guy from our sister-school who was flirting with me. He wasn't quite as charming or as handsome, but he was sweet and it felt exciting to be pursued. I wasn't used to being interesting to anyone in that way, so I decided to lean into it.

With all of the beer we were consuming, things got fairly steamy fairly quickly and, after an hour or so, we slipped outside for a few minutes alone.

We sat along the edge of a little bridge just a few steps from the pub. We were pretty buzzed and the fresh night air on our faces felt exhilarating. Our legs were dangling over the side of the bridge and the babbling sound of the rushing water was dancing around us. We continued the kissing that had started inside, and, at one point, I pulled away. I wanted to make it explicitly clear that kissing was going to be the maximum extent of our intimacy. I didn't want to be a tease or to get into an awkward situation.

He said that he was ok with that boundary, but he kept trying to take things further than a passionate make-out session. He kept running his hand up my back behind my head, and slowly leaning me down onto the ground, feeling me up, trying to get under my shirt. I kept springing back up and interrupting it with gentle pushback.

I liked the kissing, but the rest was beyond what I was willing to do.

I shut him down three times in a row and I was beginning to get irritated. The fun of the situation was quickly becoming un-fun. When he started again, a fourth time, I didn't just sit up, I stood up. I went from soft and sweet to hard and harsh. I pointed my finger at him and in a firm and defiant voice, I chided him.

"What are you doing? I've been clear about this. This is not ok. I told you I didn't want to do anything more than make out. You agreed. And now you just can't keep your hands to yourself.

"That's enough.

"You're being so ungentlemanly. Disgusting.

"I don't even want to see your face."

With that, I turned on my heels and marched myself back into the pub.

Nobody had observed our tiff, but I was embarrassed and uncomfortable.

It was out of character for me to be that harsh to anyone even if they deserved it.

And, although I was a few months shy of 21, I was sheltered and inexperienced and didn't know quite what to do next. I didn't want to rock the boat, ruin the party or start drama between our groups, so I didn't say a word to anyone about it. I just got another drink and rejoined my friends at our table.

He came in less than a minute after me and went back to his friends. He didn't say a word either.

We didn't look at one another again.

And we both proceeded to continue to drink. A lot. I drank well past my limit.

It was time for me to go home—the party wasn't done, but I was. He came over to the door and offered to walk me back to campus. I was drunk and absolutely needed help getting back. He was a nice guy. My friends had seen us making out, so they didn't think twice about it. I hadn't told them that I was angry with him and must not have said a word of protest then either. They all loved me and wouldn't have sent me off into the woods with this guy if I were protesting or hesitant in any way.

I needed to go home. They wanted to stay. He offered to walk me. It seemed like a perfect solution.

But I don't remember what I thought or what I said at that juncture. From about an hour after the bridge incident, my memories from that evening are spotty. I have a few little islands of memory surrounded by chunks of time that are absent. I've looked it up many times. It's called a brownout and is one step removed from a total blackout.

I don't remember withholding my consent and don't remember giving it.

I do know that I was firmly rooted in the belief that sex outside of marriage was wrong. Seriously wrong. Deeply sinful and I know I did not want that type of stain on my soul. I also know, with unshakable certainty that, just a few hours earlier, I hadn't even wanted to go to second base with him. And he knew it. I had made the line I was comfortable with abundantly clear verbally and nonverbally, more than once.

I was a virgin and had intended to stay that way. It was something I held sacred and special, and I certainly wouldn't ever have made the lucid choice to lose my virginity on the dirty forest floor, ripping the sarong I had borrowed, losing my underwear somewhere in the leaves, caking shoes that weren't even mine in a thick layer of mud, in a drunken stupor somewhere in the foothills of the Austrian Alps between the pub and the dorms.

But that is what happened.

Right there on the forest floor, midway back to the Kartause.

Then he escorted me back to my campus, dirty, with leaves in my hair and mud and dirt all over my clothes and my body. It was the middle of the night and he made sure to check the passageways before we went in them so nobody would see us. I was barefoot. We had spent time searching for the shoes and for my panties. He told me he would find the shoes for me the next day when it was light again.

When I woke up the next morning, my roommate was already gone, and I felt groggy. I had glimpses and clips in my mind of what had happened, but in those few hazy waking seconds, I thought it had just been a bad and very strange dream. When I pulled the sheet back, my crisp, clean, white sheets were littered with leaves and dirt. The second I saw the bedsheets and my own filthy body; I had a sinking feeling.

It wasn't a nightmare.

It was real.

The dirt in my bed, in my hair, on my sheets were the evidence of the whole traumatic event. I crawled into the shower and sat on the floor, sobbing. As the water washed away the dirt, I watched the brown water swish over my body and swirl across the white floor as it sought escape down the silver drain. I couldn't take my eyes from the swirling brown water, washing the dirt off my body. I sat on the floor of the shower for a long time letting the water run over me.

I felt so dirty.

No matter how long I spent under the water, that feeling didn't wash away.

I was too sick to wander far from my room that day and, after lunch, I was lounging on a couch in the common area just around the corner from my room. A few of my friends were chatting and one of them casually mentioned how she had seen underwear in the woods on her morning hike. She had scoffed judgmentally about how some of the students from our sister school must have had too much of a good time. I nearly sank into the floor.

She had no idea.

Shame and guilt engulfed me, and I pretended to think it was funny, too.

As soon as she left the room fear and desperation gripped me.

I had to go retrieve the evidence of what I could only see as my own sexual sin.

So, I gathered all of the emotional fortitude I had left and went in search of that pair of yellow panties with delicate pink and red flowers and slim green vines with a little white lace just around the outside edges. I found them just off the path about halfway to the pub, partially buried in the plant litter on the forest floor. I looked furtively around to be sure I wasn't observed, grabbed them guiltily and shoved them into my pocket. Now that the evidence was picked up, I realized that there should have been shoes there somewhere too. I searched in a sort of panic and couldn't find them. That's when I remembered that he had promised to get them for me.

I had a flash of "that was nice of him" flit through my brain and then I went into a numb sort of autopilot. I could only think of the shoes. I wanted my friend's shoes back. So, I went to the dorms on the other side of campus where our big-sister-school was. I had never been there before and was surprised with how different it felt on that side of the campus. It felt less idyllic and more sterile. The rooms weren't a cozy, sort-of-lodge feel, they were more like a crowded hotel with people everywhere.

It didn't take me long to find the guy's dorm and locate his specific room. When I walked in, I didn't look at him. I asked for the shoes. He talked to me as he handed them over, but I didn't hear what he was saying.

They were caked in dried mud.

I took them and quickly left.

I hardly spoke ten words.

I then retreated to our familiar side of the campus. As I walked across the huge courtyard and put distance between that set of buildings and our set, a wave of relief washed over my tense body.

The relief was short-lived. When I got back to my own room and saw my sheets, a gripping need to clean things up took hold of me. I washed the shoes, I washed the sheets, and I washed myself again. I went to bed as soon as it was dark.

When classes resumed on Monday, I continued going to classes like nothing had happened, but for nearly two weeks I avoided the one location that both schools shared: the cafeteria.

I didn't want to see him.

I felt terrible.

Physically and emotionally, I was a mess. I thought that I had had sex and lost my virginity on the forest floor. I was grieving over it. I hadn't wanted things to happen that way, but I didn't think for a second that anything more had happened. I was ashamed and sad and sick, so sick! I spent the remainder of the semester unable to hold down most food, drinking more than was reasonable, and getting weaker and sicker.

By the time I went home about eight weeks later, I was so sick that I was taken to specialist after specialist to figure out what was wrong with me. I was still not able to hold food down. I had no energy and would get exhausted and unable to function after even the slightest physical exertion. I had no idea what it was. Neither did the doctors.

I didn't, for a moment, think it had anything to do with what happened in the forest.

Eventually, I was diagnosed with a muscle virus, was given a steroid regimen and an easy-on-the systems diet and was told to rest. I did and I started to recover. I went back to my college a few weeks late to finish the second semester of my junior year. I buried myself in school and work and didn't give the events in Austria a second thought.

I just tried to move on.

I put that night into a little box in my memory and buried it deep on the shelf and it wasn't until that sunny spring afternoon, sitting on the floor of my friend's apartment, that I truly understood what had happened to me. And it took me months to reconcile that knowledge within myself and years to get help.

For a long time, I didn't get help because I didn't want to identify myself as a rape victim. What I had been through didn't feel as bad as what I had imagined rape was like. From TV and movies, I had an image in my mind that rape was physically violent, under duress, threatened by a weapon or extreme physical force, and accompanied by physical assault. And while that is certainly what has happened to many people, that wasn't what happened to me.

So, I distanced myself from the definition of being a rape victim.

And in doing that, I distanced myself from the help that I could have had.

You see, when you have a definition of something and you can warp the definition enough so that you don't fit within its boundaries, you can allow yourself to stand outside of it, avoid the reality of it, and ignore its huge implications in your life.

It's a psychological protection mechanism that allows you to stay within your status quo—no matter how bad it may be—and not have to feel the consequence of being included in the definition.

For example, if you are someone who gets drunk every night and is totally dependent upon drinking every day, you are an alcoholic. But if you've convinced yourself that an alcoholic is someone who drinks by themselves and you never do that, you don't have to accept the label and the ensuing consequences. If you then start to drink when you're alone and shift the line in your mind to say that an alcoholic is actually someone who drinks at work and you don't do that, then once again you dodge the whole train. Then if you start to spike your morning coffee and tuck a flask in the glove compartment of your car for an afternoon top-off, you might move the boundary again and say, well an alcoholic is someone who gets violent when they drink and no matter that you drink every day, and while you're alone, and while you're at work, you still don't get violent when you drink and can count yourself safe from the definition of an alcoholic and all of its ramifications.

Shifting the boundaries of what we think something is so that we are outside of that boundary is a dangerous and slippery slope—one that I lived on for a long time.

I accepted that I had been raped, but I did not see myself as a rape victim.

Several years elapsed.

It had been four and half years since that Halloween party and the subsequent trauma. I had self-medicated with oh-so-much sex and alcohol and work obsession for years.

But it wasn't enough anymore.

There was a wounded part of me that I couldn't fix by avoiding it, by pretending it didn't exist, by shoving it down. It was staring me in the face and the more I grew in awareness of who I was, the more I looked to my talents and sought to strengthen them, the more I embraced personal growth, the more conscious I became that I wasn't really as ok as I pretended to be.

And I remember the moment that all started to change.

I was dating a man 18 years my senior. Tall, handsome, with the sexiest French accent. He saw me and cherished me in a way that I hadn't ever experienced before. He saw me for who I was, and for who I could become. Under his gaze, for the first time in my whole life, I felt truly beautiful.

One evening we were talking about my personal development journey. He knew about my rape and about the wild and wandering ways I had self-medicated around it. He knew I had been trying to heal from it, pursuing personal development paths, leaning on my Faith. And that night he told me that he admired me for the work I had put into healing. He gave me credit for all I had done, all of the effort I had put into reconciling that trauma within myself.

He told me that I had done all I could do to heal on my own and that it was time for me to seek some professional help.

"You need it," he said. "You deserve it."

You deserve it.

Those words touched me. My heart, which had been hardened against the idea of seeking therapy, melted. I felt held, supported, seen.

My body physically relaxed.

The serious look on my face gave way to a bright and shining smile.

I could feel a wave of relief wash over my tired soul.

Although we rarely talked about it in my family, I had this vague feeling that therapy was something that only the weak sought, only the broken or the self-indulgent pursued. It had always smacked of something somewhat shameful.

And those three words dissolved all that in an instant.

You deserve it.

I deserved it.

I had earned it. I merited it. This was not some shameful curse but a prize, a gift, a privilege—and one that I was ready for, that was owed to me.

Therapy was not and is not something reserved for the weak. In fact, weakness could not be further from the truth.

Therapy requires courage.

You have to be willing to talk about the event itself, to explore the impact that it made, to discuss the shadow that's cast by what I call the Lightning Rod Moment.

Lightning Rod Moments are the events in our life that strike us to the core and have a deep and lasting impact upon us, upon the way we see ourselves and the world around us.

These moments can be obviously traumatic or they can be seemingly small and insignificant. Regardless of how they may appear, their unifying factor is that they are always significant and deeply impactful to us.

Their shadows are long and their ripples are wide.

They have a truly outsized impact on our lives.

Imagine that your life is a track. How you live determines whether the track goes round and round and round and round without changing in size or elevation or whether it starts out small and radiates into higher and bigger circles as time progresses.

Each year that passes has the potential to take us up the ascent to a new level and a wider band. When you choose to live your life without growth, however, you stay on the same familiar, predictable, well-trodden track. When you embrace growth, the familiar track breaks free from its bindings, slopes upwards and starts to expand.

When a Lightning Rod Moment occurs, it's as though a dense, dark rod implants itself across the span of our track. The rod shoots up into the space above, getting fainter and less dense as it rises. As we navigate the course of our life, we intersect the rods again and again.

There is no getting around them.

If you are fixed in your trajectory, you will bump into those rods and will relive their trauma over and over in new and varied ways. They feel inescapable and their reverberations seem to follow endlessly.

If, however, you are on a growth trajectory and you have put in the work to face the trauma, and lessen its impact on your life, you will intersect with it again, but the rod will be less dense, the impact less and less dramatic until eventually, the rod dissipates and no longer has a trace on your ascending track.

As the lighting rod fades, the shock and trauma fade with it and all that is left is the gift it contained hiding, very well hidden, in the hideous wrapping paper of the striking event.

We all have these lightning rod moments.

Some of us have only one or two while others have many. They can happen at any age and at any moment.

Hiding from them does not make them go away. Ignoring them doesn't change them one bit. They only start to disappear when we put in the work to look them in the eye and reconcile them within the greater story of our lives.

And so often that requires professional help and seeking that help is not easy. It requires immense courage and emotional fortitude.

There might be pain. There might be threads woven together that are difficult to untwine. There might be unconscious behaviors at work or disempowering stories running behind the scenes. You have to be willing to confront it all. The pain, the discomforts, the misalignment—all of it.

But when you can summon the courage and seek the support and do the work, you can learn to look for the gift that was bestowed.

Because there is always a gift, no matter how ugly the wrapping paper that contained it.

And that gift is not freely given. It is found. It is earned.

THE MIRROR EXERCISE

♥

Several years ago I heard a speaker say from the stage that her services were totally worth it *"at full price."* I was not only impressed by her bold, confident style but I was also inspired with a new tool to support the many sales teams I trained. Her statement gave me simple but powerful language to see whether my trainees believed in their worth or not.

I've used it thousands of times, with great success.

And we can easily adapt this to our deep work here too. This is how.

Stand in front of the mirror.

Look yourself squarely in the eye and say: "I love and accept myself exactly as I am in this moment, inside and out."

And then pause. Take a few deep breaths. Scan your body from head to toe and see if there is any discomfort internally or externally. Did speaking those words make you feel reassured? Peaceful? Calm? Did they ring true? Or did they feel foreign, or false, or disingenuous?

When we have gone through trauma, it can distort our vision of ourselves and we may need a little extra help in getting to or back to a place of self-love. I know it was a long journey for me!

So if you try that approach and it doesn't leave you feeling calm and settled, pull out a piece of paper and write down three things that you like about yourself. Three genuine aspects of yourself that you can unreservedly love. Maybe it's your body, your skin, your hair, your feet, your fingers, your smile. Maybe it's your character, or your sense of humor, or your style. Maybe it's the way you do good in the world around you or the care you take of your family.

No matter what, there are three things.

Find them and be as specific as you can.

Repeat the exercise daily until you start to believe the words you spoke in the mirror. Or, if you're more like me, just keep writing and writing until you run out of paper and, if you still don't feel them ringing true, write just a little bit more.

Know that you are worthy of love, acceptance, honoring.

You deserve it.

Always.

Take things deeper at:
www.madeleinemacrae.com/gifts

♡ Madeleine

CHAPTER 7

RADICLE GRATITUDE

"Quantum Physicists are not exactly sure what happens when the wave becomes a particle... but they are all agreed on one thing, that reality comes into being through an interaction, and so do you."

— EMILY LEVINE

I WAS QUIETLY SMILING AS I GLANCED AROUND HER OFFICE.

T HERE WAS A SMALL sculpture on the built-in mahogany shelves to my right. The sculpture was made of two intertwining circles and was no more than eight or nine inches tall. The circles had varying depth and went from broad to narrow in an undulating sort of motion. Their smooth curves blended into each other at their one point of intersection. The silver looked soft to the touch.

It comforted me.

I had come to her office that afternoon because I was ready. Ready to heal from the extreme impact of having been violated. No longer did I need to allow the reverberations of that dark night in Austria to extend and ripple over the track of my life. It was time. Time to reach out for help. I knew I needed it and the doorway of willingness to get it was unlocked in my heart when I realized that I deserved it. I didn't have to accept a life overshadowed by the impact of trauma.

It was mid 2008.

A few weeks prior I had finally been ready.

And when I'm ready, I go full tilt. So, I looked for the fastest and best path to the outcome I was looking to achieve. I didn't want to sit in an office and have endless conversations about my feelings. I just wanted to figure out how to fix what had broken inside of me when I was raped and to move forward with my life.

I wanted to be free.

After some searching, I found an innovative way of working through a traumatic event in an intensive session that helped the person see and experience the traumatic situation through a whole new lens. It promised big results and fast. That was exactly what I wanted, so I combed through the list of practitioners in and around southern Florida where I lived at the time, and I found a female therapist who had a long and impressive career helping professional people with their personal problems—particularly with sexual trauma.

That was me.

I filled out the form and booked the session.

Naively, I thought I would waltz on in there and we would get down to the business of clearing away the rape trauma immediately.

That is not what happened.

In our first session, my therapist—a wise old woman with white-ish grey hair and a kind and gentle voice—explained to me how my subconscious mind worked.

As I sat on the comfortable couch across from her in her brown leather chair studded with nail heads, she told me that the subconscious doesn't function within the framework of time. She described it like a sandy beach that has just been saturated with water. It's jiggly and impressionable. If you hit your hand really hard on the sand, the handprint will just stay there. It won't wash away until the water comes over it again.

But our subconscious doesn't have a tide or water. It's just eternally jiggly, impressionable sand.

I was fascinated. I hung on her every word.

She had me think of a time when I had seen a grown person act like a child. An example popped into my mind immediately. There were tons of them. She said that when trauma happens to us it's like a big, huge hand slaps the sand of our subconscious mind and leaves a deep imprint. From that point forward, every time we encounter something that's similar in some way to that trauma, we go and stand inside of the indent of the imprint and revert back to behavioral patterns that would have been appropriate at the age we were when the trauma occurred.

Trauma, she told me, resides in the subconscious mind and stays in an eternally present moment, putting us back in that moment when we are triggered.

The mind candy of this new information was delicious, and I was enjoying it immensely. She let me soak it in as I looked around her beautiful office. It was then that I noticed the sculpture nestled amid the high-end finishes and the expensive furniture. These furnishings told me that she had been very successful, and I felt lucky to be sitting there with her, in such capable and experienced hands.

She went on to explain that her process was akin to pouring water over the handprint. We would let the water flow until the imprint lost its form and the sand was smooth again.

I was ready and eager to get started.

She didn't ask me what the trauma was that had brought me to her, but it was detailed in the form I filled out prior to booking our appointment, so she knew what I wanted to resolve. She told me that we weren't going to start there, and a wave of disappointment swept over me. She said that we were going to work on something smaller today to help me get a feel for what the therapeutic process was like before we tackled the bigger issue.

The disappointment gave way to a little bit of worry. My body felt sweaty, and I started to feel my stomach churn a bit. Although ready for it, I was still a little intimidated by therapy and this was a curveball. I wasn't ready for it. I hadn't prepared another topic; I hadn't thought of any other traumas. My mind started to race over my past to see if I could find something to work on.

I saw a bit of a smile creep over her face. Her eyes softened and she told me to take a deep breath. She knew that my mind was racing.

"It's ok," she said. "Your subconscious mind is wiser than you know. Take a deep breath and allow your mind to drift back and forth over the span of your past. Don't worry. Just breathe. Your mind will present exactly the right thing for us to work on. Just relax and let it pop up to the surface."

My heart rate slowed down a little bit.

I took a few long, deep breaths.

I kept breathing and scanning my own personal history.

And then it happened.

A situation jumped out at me from sixth grade.

She was right. It had just jumped right out.

My face must have lit up like a Christmas tree because she said, "You see it, don't you?"

I did.

She asked me to tell her about it.

In sixth grade I was bullied terribly. I was going to school at a tiny school started by my parent's church. There were six people in my grade and fewer than thirty-five students in between kindergarten and eighth grade. It was more of a formalized homeschool than a true academic institution.

There was one boy in my class who was incredibly mean to me day after day. Let's call him Nick.

I had a big brown birthmark on my forehead. It was sort of an oval shape, like a quarter with the sides smashed in by one of those coin flattening machines, and it held a prominent space on the upper right side of my forehead.

It was a birthmark, so I had been born that way.

And I was never self-conscious about it or ashamed of it in any way... at least not until sixth grade.

Years prior, my parents and I had toyed with having it removed but I didn't want to be in the hospital overnight and my parents weren't going to force me to have a strictly cosmetic surgery. All of our dermatologists said it was fine to keep it, so I did!

It was my choice and I kind of liked it.

It made me different, but in a special way, not a bad way.

Well, Nick did not like it. He hated it. He thought it was ugly and looked like a dirt smudge—or a poop smudge, depending on how cruel he was that day—on my face. Every day for months on end he would tease me about it on the playground. Teachers and recess monitors never stopped him, my friends never stopped him, and I tried to act like it hardly bothered me at all. Sometimes I would retaliate and defend myself, other times I would sort of laugh along, and yet other times I wouldn't respond at all, but I never let him see just how much his ugly comments really hurt.

I would come home after school, go to my room, write in my journal about it and cry.

The scene that popped into my head that afternoon on the therapist's supple brown leather couch was one particularly painful memory.

We had been playing baseball after school and he had tormented me about my poop-stain mercilessly throughout the game. Every time someone slid into first, he would taunt me. I was atypically quiet on the way home and immediately retreated to my room when I got there.

A while later, my Mom happened upon me and when she saw my tear-stained face, she demanded to know what had happened.

Now, my mom is not one to make trouble. She respects authority and has a keen sense of justice. She had been involved in the school from day one and knew all of the administrators and teachers personally. It was a small community. She was appalled to know that this had been going on for months and nobody had come to my protection or had come to her about it.

She was angry, I could tell. But I somehow felt that she was angry at me—angry that I hadn't told her sooner. She said she would take care of this with the tone of voice that brooked no opposition. I could feel her resolve but I didn't quite know what she was going to do.

The next morning it was her turn to be unusually quiet.

We went about our routine but this time, rather than dropping me off in the parking lot, she parked and came in with me. I went to class, and she marched down to the principal's office.

She told him everything.

Nick was immediately pulled from class.

I was pulled from class.

We both had to talk about what had been going on and the story wasn't a pretty one.

He was suspended for a week.

And his punishment was not only to miss school and get zeros on all work (which he still had to complete), but it also included an element of restitution towards me. He wasn't allowed to return to school until he wrote and then read a personal apology note to me in front of the school during the school assembly. Mom had argued that his offense had been public, and his apology needed to be public too. The administration agreed.

So, he did it. He wrote me a full, complete, sincere apology and read it aloud, in the chapel, in front of the entire school.

And I had never felt more vindicated in my whole life. I was glad he had been humiliated like that. He deserved it.

When I first told the therapist the story, I was still very much hurt over the whole thing. I felt that I had been left unprotected, my friends didn't stand up for me, and I definitely didn't see my mom as the heroine that she truly was. I still felt her anger had been directed at me, not at the real perpetrator.

The therapist had me retell the story slowly and we broke it down into five distinct parts. We labeled each part and she had me tell the story over and over again. Sometimes she asked me to describe what I was feeling in each part and at other times, we went into the facts.

When she snapped her fingers, we would progress to the next part of the story.

Some of the descriptions were long and she asked me all of the details; other times the descriptions were super quick before she snapped, and I had to move on. She let some of the emotional descriptions go on for a while and others were just one word before she snapped those fingers and we moved onto the next scene.

There didn't seem to be a rhyme or rhythm to what part of the story would get the long bits and what part would be short, but we went over and over it.

And the most amazing thing happened.

When we had started, my whole body had been tense. I used short, sharp, direct words. I was highly emotionally charged. I clenched my fists, held back tears and sometimes even struggled to find the words.

And as we went on, my body relaxed, the muscles in my arms relaxed, and my fingers unclenched. I felt lighter and looser. My word choice was softer.

She told me that this was going to be the last time we went over the story, and I was shocked when we got to that final scene in the chapel, with Nick standing there in front of the school assembly, looking contrite and sad.

The first time we had reviewed that scene she had asked me to share a few words that described my emotions and I had said things like revenge, triumphant, vindicated. I felt like he had gotten what he deserved and I was glad to watch him face his own shame. I was gloating over his public punishment and was delighting in it, but without any joy or peace.

But on this round, this final round, I didn't feel any of that anymore.

You see, in telling the story over and over, under her expert guidance, I realized that Nick never bullied anyone ever again after that day. I realized just what a powerful advocate my mom had been for me. How her anger wasn't at me, but at the school and at Nick. I hadn't been abandoned. She stood up for me in a big way.

She protected me.

She made sure I had a full and dramatic public apology.

I felt how much I had been loved, supported, protected.

I also felt the significance of my impact on his life. For the first time ever, I realized I had been a conduit of personal transformation for him.

When we were at the tail end of our session and we finally reached that final scene in the chapel, she asked me how I felt. I said, loved and happy. Not in a gloating and vindicated sort of way, but in a peaceful way. I had been the conduit of conversion for this boy and this situation changed the course of his life for the better. I could see the good that had come of my personal pain, and it felt really beautiful.

And the good eclipsed the pain so much that I only felt the warm glow of joy and peace radiating from that situation.

In just two short hours, I went from feeling spiteful and vengeful to feeling truly grateful. And from that moment forward, that feeling has never dissipated.

This incredible therapy session removed the handprint and forever attached positive emotions to that whole dramatic series of events.

If she could do so much for me with that painful situation from my childhood, imagine what she helped me do with the trauma of the rape.

A few weeks later when we had our multi-hour, deep dive session to help me confront and heal from that complicated and shameful violation, I walked out of her office a totally different person.

Being raped was bad.

It had hurt me for a long time, but it never hurt me in the same way again after that day.

While it undoubtedly had had some big negative ripple effects on my life, it also forced me to confront myself and to engage with myself at a deeper level.

It made me seek healing.

It made me choose what I wanted to feel and how I wanted to be in this world.

And I chose peace.

I chose gratitude.

Gratitude is not easy, but it is always, always an option.

When tragedy, trauma or tribulations strike their reverberating rod into the track of our life, it's very natural, very human, to get thrown off balance and become angry, disappointed, resentful.

To be perturbed.

Trauma, and even the more minor disruptions of our day force us to recalibrate—whether by a little or by a lot—and to rethink what we thought we were going to be doing. And the process of adaptation requires much of us.

Our plans are the connective tissue uniting our intentions to our actions and we are deeply attached to them.

We crafted them for a purpose and when we are forced to reshape, rethink and sometimes even relinquish our plans, it can be terribly hard to do.

As humans, we are physical beings imbued with spirit. While we are living our embodied existence on the physical plane here on earth, we fall under the classification of being mammals. We have a backbone, warm blood, and hair, and we produce milk to feed our babies.

It is a biological imperative that we care for offspring.

If we don't care for them, feed them, shelter them, nurture them, they won't survive. Humans aren't like reptiles who can pop out of their shells and search out their first meals by instinct alone. We have to be taught how to survive, how to thrive, and in order to reach the age to learn all that, our offspring first have to be cared for, protected, nurtured, loved.

It is in our nature.

And the plans that we hold for ourselves are the offspring of our hearts and minds.

We love them greatly. We cherish them. And we have to be looking for a higher good, a greater good, in order to find the courage to override that instinct to blindly protect them and instead, to be flexible with our plans, to adjust in the face of the unforeseen, to reroute.

Setting aside what you thought you were going to be doing, whether in the macro plan of your life or the micro plan of your day, can be hard and sometimes even turbulent. And one of the most helpful resources to move from perturbation to peace is gratitude. Gratitude can be absolutely life-changing.

A few years ago, I was visiting a dear friend of mine. We were sitting outside, admiring the beautiful flowers in her backyard and chatting. As I looked over at her, I realized that Ann was the happiest, calmest, most peaceful I had seen her in nearly a decade.

I didn't vocalize it in that moment because even the thought took me by surprise.

It was only a year or so prior that we had sat across the table from each other at dinner and had talked about the deep struggle she was having in her marriage. She and her husband weren't communicating well, weren't supporting each other as they both needed, and were losing their connection. She had confided in me how scary and painful it was for her. She had been married for nearly a decade and was always intensely private and discreet about her relationship struggles, so I knew that things had to be bad—really bad—for her to tell me about it that evening.

I'll never forget when she said, "I hate to think of where the road that we are on is going to lead." I didn't know what to tell her. I had no good ideas on how to get her husband to change, how to make things better in their marriage, and my heart broke for my sweet friend.

Fast-forward sixteen months. It was day three of my trip and I could see that things in their relationship hadn't changed substantially. The issues that had been bothering Ann back then were clearly still an issue.

Yet, here she was, sitting in the sunshine, gently looking after her children, chatting with me, looking truly content and thriving.

Throughout the rest of my trip, I continued to observe her newfound sense of self and of hope and of happiness every day. I was overjoyed for her. Her situation hadn't changed—in fact it had intensified in some ways—but she was different than she had been before. She was peaceful and truly content.

I flew home determined to discover her secret.

A few weeks after that trip, Ann and I were chatting on the phone. Her kids were napping, and I thought it was the perfect time to delve into this mystery. I brought it up gently but directly—in my signature style—and she said something that shocked me.

"You know, I was really unhappy for a long time. I was starting to consider worst case scenarios when I reached out for some help.

"I have a therapist that I go to see now and then and when I told her how unhappy my husband was making me, she told me: 'Ann, your happiness is your own responsibility.'

"That idea had never crossed my mind before. I had been living like it was his responsibility to make me happy and when I realized that my happiness wasn't his job, I also realized that I was the only one who could make this situation better for myself.

"If I kept dwelling on all of the things that my husband was doing wrong, all of the ways he wasn't fulfilling my needs, all of the ways that I needed support from him and wasn't getting it, we were on the fast path to nowhere good.

"So, on the advice of my therapist, I decided to make my happiness my own job."

As she was speaking, my eyes closed. I had my bare toes on the textured wooden floor below me, gently pushing myself back and forth on the cozy, round, swivel rocker I was in, and I was soaking in her every word.

I was fascinated. I hadn't ever heard it put that way before.

My happiness is my own job.

My responsibility.

Mine.

Not anyone else no matter how close or committed they may be to me.

It was like tasting deeply satisfying mind candy and I had to know more. "That's amazing. I haven't heard that before either. It seems obvious now that you've said it, but I have never consciously expressed that to myself before.

"So, what did you do?"

"I learned how to dig deep and be grateful. It was the only tool that my therapist gave me that day, and I wanted to save my marriage, so I decided to try it."

She told me that her therapist wanted her to find one thing about her husband every single day to be grateful for. One thing, no matter how big or how small, to genuinely appreciate. "And," she added, "I had to voice that appreciation out loud—not to my husband, but just to myself.

"And that part was so critical. Hearing it said, out loud, was part of what made it so powerful. I wasn't just thinking it, I was saying it. Saying it to myself and to my kids."

She acknowledged that it was incredibly hard at first.

She was hurt and angry and resentful and it took all of her mental strength to find one thing every day. She was so used to seeing only his faults and failures that finding something to be grateful for about her husband took conscious effort, and sticking with it took a determination of will that she had to tap into every day anew.

She told me that she started small, and she started slow.

When she would trip on his shoes in the middle of the room, she would stop herself from feeling frustrated and her efforts at organization, thwarted. She would make a conscious decision to be grateful instead and she would say aloud, "I'm so grateful that he was here."

When he wouldn't answer her calls, she would have to decide not to go down the familiar route of feeling unimportant and ignored and unsupported and would choose instead to speak the words, "Well, I'm glad he is busy at work. He's making a living that's taking care of our needs. I'm grateful for that."

At first, her gratitudes were basic and begrudging.

But she made it her mission to find things to be grateful for, and to say them out loud every day.

Her verbalization wasn't for him, her verbalization was for herself and for her children. They all needed to hear it, to feel it, to think it—to allow the spoken words to carve a new path in their minds and in their hearts.

When the kids would complain that their dad wasn't home for dinner, she would make a game of finding all of the hidden ways he was actually there—in the food he paid for, in the chairs, the table, the silverware. The kids loved it and they actively participated in finding gratitude hiding in places they hadn't ever looked before.

As time wore on, she was able to find more and more things to be genuinely grateful for. She went from struggling to find one thing in a day to finding many things all day long, effortlessly, to be grateful to have, to be grateful to be.

Nothing was too small and nothing was too big to escape the reach of her gratitude.

As she started to fixate on what was beautiful again, she started to feel a little better and started to make space in her life for more of the things she loved—time with friends, fine art, music, books.

Even some of the things that used to feel like chores she had to shoulder alone became sources of joy, like creating delicious food to feed her family, or finding ways to make harmony in her home. She filled up her own cup. She took her happiness as her own responsibility.

She did this for a year.

One whole year.

And during that year her life changed.

And she found that there was still something beautiful in her marriage, something empowering to discover, something worth staying and working for.

She found beautiful things about her spouse.

She found beautiful things about herself.

And as she discovered all of this beauty in and around her, she found herself feeling more content, more cognizant of the good, more empowered, free, hopeful. Nothing had changed with her husband. He was still the same as the year prior, but she had changed, and her transformation impacted not only what she saw going on around her, but how she felt about it.

She had agency again.

She was in control of her own feelings and took ownership of her own happiness. Her cup was full and was filling itself from the inside out. She was living congruently with who she was as a person and found peace in doing that.

It was like she had gotten her master's degree in gratitude, and it had transformed her life.

And her story that afternoon transformed me too.

I had never thought of gratitude as a chosen habit and was deeply struck by it all and by the incredible outcome it produced in her life.

I've shared Ann's story many times with clients, with friends, with people who were stuck, and it's transformed their lives too.

And I call what she did going on a journey of Radicle Gratitude.

I love that name because it sounds like radical—a term I always associate with amazing excellence (I am a child of the '80s after all!)—and that fits, but it also means something so much deeper.

The radicle, in botany, is the first organ that develops when a seed starts to germinate—the very first little part that bursts out of the seed. It digs downward into the soil and holds the seed still like an anchor, as all of the beautiful flora pushes up from the soil and the plant grows and blooms.

And that's what she did.

She planted the anchoring root of gratitude in her life and in her marriage.

She embraced *Radicle* Gratitude—down to the tiniest root—and it allowed the flower to blossom again, more beautifully than ever before.

You see, no matter what the circumstances of our life deal us, we can decide how we narrate the story, we can choose to look for more empowering details, we can decide to seek peace through the doorway of gratitude.

When we recognize that we are the ones who have the power to change our own narrative and when we have the courage to do it, transformation has the space to happen.

Ann and I both chose to confront the painful parts of our lives, not to let the pain get in the way of our course towards a thriving today and a thriving tomorrow. We both found the courage to seek a way through the pain and into healing. We both looked the lighting rod moments in our lives directly in the eye and found our way to a deeper peace than either of us had ever known.

Our willing confrontation of the unacceptable, the uncomfortable and our determined pursuit of peace led us down paths we hadn't intended to travel, and we wrote a new narrative. Those once nearly tragic stories transformed before our eyes into anchors holding us steady so we could grow and blossom and be fruitful.

The tether of radicle gratitude grounded us, rooted us, nourished us and helped to heal us too.

21 DAY CHALLENGE

—————————— ♥ ——————————

Gratitude is often mistaken for willful blindness—closing your eyes to what really is and reinventing a world where the bad things aren't quite so bad, the ugly situations maybe a little less hideous, the hard soul-crushing realities of our lives just little bumps along the way.

But that is not gratitude at all. That's an unhealthy blend of denial and minimization.

Gratitude is not blind.

Gratitude is seeing the world for what is—being deeply realistic—and making an act of the will, a clear and intentional choice to focus on the good and the beautiful.

It is not putting lipstick on a pig.

It's seeing the pig, smelling the smell of the sty, knowing that the pig will eat every and any leftover or scrap you send its way and that it will roll around in its own muck and mud too. And rather than trying to make the pig neat and tidy, rather than putting all of your focus and attention on the stench, it's accepting the piggy mess, allowing the smell to be there without complaining and fussing over it, and appreciating that loud, messy, smelly creature for recycling what would have become refuse.

True gratitude seeks the good despite the wrapping paper.

And today I want to invite you to immerse yourself in gratitude. To choose optimism. Optimism and gratitude are habits of thought. And no matter your past, your predispositions or your current path, you too can cultivate them.

Join the millions of people who have felt the transformational power of optimism.

To get you started on this journey or to deepen your current sense of gratitude, I've designed a **21-Day Radicle Challenge** just for you!

I'll see you there!

Join our 21 Day Challenge at:
www.madeleinemacrae.com/gifts

♡ Madeleine

CHAPTER 8

LETTING GO

"Fire converts all things into fire."

— ST. JOHN OF THE CROSS

THE AIR WAS FRESH. THE GRASS, BRIGHT GREEN.

M Y SIBLINGS AND I were out in the country spending time with a few of our family friends. It was summertime between my third and fourth grade years and we hadn't seen our friends in weeks—which in kid years felt like decades. They lived a solid ninety minutes away in a beautiful, lush part of Michigan, thirty minutes north of the school that my Mom used to drive us to daily.

I grew up in the suburbs outside of the Detroit airport. I was staunchly blue collar and definitively not a country girl, so all of the games that my friends played were fascinating and fun: hide-and-go-seek in the hayloft, corn tag, and, on this particular afternoon, crack the whip.

It was electrifying.

Literally, electrifying.

To play the game, you had to hold hands in a big, long row and run around with the leader determining where the trailing group would go. Eventually, after many circles and winding shapes, the leader of the line would grab the electric fence that kept the docile cows happily grazing in their field. When the leader grabbed the wire, the daisy chain of hands formed a circuit, and the electric current would run through everyone and would only zap the very last person in the line, the one acting as the ground. The settings on the electric fence were low, but the electric current pulsing through the fence was enough to give you a strong zap if you weren't paying attention.

While we didn't know the physics of it at the time, we did know that if you were fast enough letting go of the hand of the person in front of you, you wouldn't feel the shock at all; but if you were slow, you sure would feel it.

And when that happened, it was not pleasant.

It hurt.

There was only one rule in the game. You couldn't let go of the hand in front of you until the person behind you let go of your hand. If you let go too soon, you would be eliminated and would have to sit out the next round. The point was to be the last person standing, aside from the leader.

And that was the coveted position: the leader.

The leader would try to fake everyone out. They would run close to the fence and reach out their free hand only to whizz past and keep the line in motion. They wanted to try to grab that thin piece of wire while everyone else was preoccupied by all the twists and turns they had made to trick people into letting go too early. Ideally the leader would grab the fence while everyone was still running around like a long human piece of rope, unaware that the current was now active through the chain.

So, everyone had to keep their eye on the leader and be ready to let go like a big row of incredibly quick dominos.

The game wasn't without its risk and despite all of that—or maybe because the danger made it more exhilarating—we loved it.

And that afternoon was the first time I had ever played.

There were a good dozen of us involved in the game. I was among the youngest of the players and the eldest were high school-aged boys. Everyone, except myself and my two siblings, the city slickers as they called us, had played this game many times. They were country kids. Tough and strong and hearty.

I spent a few rounds in the middle of the chain and had beginner's luck on my side. I hadn't gotten zapped or eliminated yet. I was feeling pretty proud of myself. It took a huge dose of courage to jump into the game in the first place, but with each round that didn't result in a negative outcome, my confidence grew.

I thought I was ready to give the end of the line a try. They hadn't let me be at the end in the first few rounds because they thought it would be too hard for me and that I would get hurt. But I was bold by this time. I felt invincible. I felt that my sharp eyes could keep track of the wily leader and that my winning streak would continue.

They relented.

So, we all grabbed hands and started the mad dash around the field again. We were going so fast. My heart was pounding more in terror now than in joy. I was going faster than my two feet had ever carried me before. I was hardly even making contact with the grass beneath my blue and white tennis shoes.

We were twisting and turning and the line felt like it had a life of its own. The leader made a sharp angled turn and the front of the line was doubling back, running nearly parallel to the back half of the line with my little body at the tail end. As one of the older boys in the middle reached that pivot point, he planted his feet like an anchor and the momentum jerked to a halt.

The trailing group of us whipped around, hard, and a few of us went flying.

I was so light that the sudden shift in momentum swept me right off my feet and flung me across the yard, thankfully, right into a soft pile of unbaled hay. I was a little shocked and shaken but not hurt.

The others were too.

I had let go of the hand in front of me.

Two other people had as well.

We were out.

I was disappointed to be disqualified, but inwardly, I was grateful for the rest and was pretty happy that I hadn't gotten zapped yet either. That little moment of flight had been quite enough excitement for me for a little while and I was content watching from the sidelines.

The sun was dancing on the grass and made each blade look like its own vibrant piece of carefully crafted art. As I sat there with my pretty floral dress spread around me like its own type of flower in the grass, I soaked in the beauty and the boisterous glee of the game.

That big boy who had done the anchor stunt ended up winning and the next game was about to begin. I snapped out of my tranquil rest, shot up like a bullet and shouted "Dibs!" as I made my way back into the group.

"What do you mean, dibs?" one of the bigger boys sort of jeered.

"I mean, I call front of the line."

They all looked at me with a mixture of surprise and disbelief, with a smidge of respect in there too. They were a little impressed that such a little girl made so bold a claim. Three of the boys were high schoolers, big, strong, athletic and here I was, a wisp of a fourth grader, ready to be in control of the game.

A debate began that devolved into me begging them to let me be at the front of the line next. They had absolutely rejected the idea at first but were starting to show signs of giving way as my persistent pleading continued.

Anticipatory adrenaline pulsed through my veins.

They were about to give me a turn at the front.

That's when one of the older girls, who had been watching from afar, came running up and intervened. She insisted that I not be allowed to be the leader of the line.

"Maddie, that fence is going to kick your butt. We've been playing forever, and we know how to touch the wire so that it doesn't hurt too bad. You have to be fast. Really fast and if you do it wrong, Maddie, you're going to be crying and you might get hurt bad. It's not worth it. Just have fun. Maybe when you've played a few more times, and you're a bit older, you can have a turn being the leader."

My pride was hurt.

It was common knowledge that athletics weren't my greatest gift. I was always one of the last ones to be picked for any sort of game that required speed or agility. I didn't love that, but I also knew it to be true.

I wasn't fast.

And if success at the front of the line required speed, I was bound to fail.

I knew it as soon as she said it. And, the more I thought about it, the less I liked the idea of being zapped to the point of tears in front of all of my friends. So I let her sound reasoning win me over and I relinquished my contention for the top spot without much pushback.

That older girl showed great compassion in not letting me grab a hold of that wire that afternoon.

She knew something I didn't know.

She knew the secret of the game.

She knew that the leader grabbed the fence, but they didn't hold on. As soon as the line of people started to dwindle, they would slowly uncurl their fingers so that only a fingertip was on the wire at the very end. When it was their turn to let go, they would just back away from the fence and break the tie nice and easy.

No zap.

It was subtle and nobody caught on. Only those who knew, knew.

If you were standing there with your fingers gripping the wire, you would get zapped. And as that shocking pain went through your body, it became harder and harder to unwrap your fingers and let go of the fence.

While the game was mostly for fun, it could be a mean way to haze cocky city kids, so when I discovered their secret many years later, I was grateful that I hadn't been allowed to grab hold of the wire.

Crack the whip made a huge impression on me, and that sunny afternoon has been played and replayed in my memory hundreds of times over.

The symbolism it carries is profound.

There have been so many times in my life that things were causing me pain and they just kept on being painful over and over and over. It felt like they were gripping me, holding me, wrapping me tightly. I felt bound by them.

But the more I confronted them, the more closely I observed my own thoughts and behaviors, the more I uncovered the hidden drivers behind my behaviors. And I realized the thing causing me pain was not holding me, I was holding it.

The pain could stop if I unclenched my grip.

There is a beautiful Buddhist teaching about physical pain. It says that physical pain is like an arrow. It pierces and hurts. But if we allow our physical pain to put us in emotional anguish, it's like being shot with a second arrow. And the second is more painful than the first.

I think of that second arrow as keeping hold of the electric fence. When something that has happened to us in our lives is causing us ongoing, active pain, it's a sign that we are not yet fully healed from it.

And you have to exit the pain, survive that painful part, before you can start the bigger work of healing.

I'll never forget the day I learned that lesson.

It was the day I gave birth to my son.

Paul and I had gotten up before the break of dawn to make the forty-five-minute drive to the hospital to be on time for an early morning induction.

Noah, in his signature style, was comfy and cozy right where he was, and was showing no signs whatsoever of being willing to leave his home in my womb. My due date had come and gone and, as a first-time mother, my doctors were anxious that I not go too far beyond a week overdue, so I was scheduled for an induction.

Now, I had been the happiest pregnant person on the face of the planet. Despite horrific morning sickness for many long months, I had walked around on cloud nine for all the months. I couldn't wait to be a mom. It was something that I had always wanted.

My pregnancy was highly unexpected but by no means unwanted.

I was excited for the baby and I'll be the first to admit that I was woefully unprepared for birth.

I hadn't toured the hospital or done birthing classes or anything like that.

I just decided to wing it.

By the end of my pregnancy, I was huge and tired and just ready to be done being pregnant. I didn't want to do more than I absolutely had to do, so I didn't. By that point, even my happiness was being stretched to its limit.

While I didn't do the typical preparations, I didn't do nothing to prepare. I read a book or two and had lots of conversations with my doctors. I had a plan and I thought that I was prepared.

I was not.

When we arrived at the hospital I remember feeling a sense of awe and relief as Paul and I walked down the long, white, brightly lit corridor from the check-in desk to our birthing suite.

The air in the hospital was cool.

We got to our room and things felt a little anticlimactic. We had hurried to arrive on time, rushed through the paperwork, and then I had got all dressed into the gown and situated on the bed only to wait and wait and wait.

The minutes ticking by felt so long and I started to focus on the space around me. The room felt sterile, and I was surprised that it wasn't more inviting. This was a huge moment in my life, and I would have liked a little nicer environment.

A wave of regret for not having toured the birthing wing swept over me.

But before I had time to indulge in that disempowering line of thinking the nurses came in to run all their day-of tests. It wasn't too long before they brought the Pitocin that was going to entice my body to go into labor.

I thought labor would come on quickly, but it didn't.

We had another long period of waiting and it was late in the morning before anything at all started to happen.

I was drifting in and out of sleep when suddenly the contractions started to grip my whole body.

Natural contractions, uninduced, undulate like a big wave slowly increasing in intensity, peaking and then diminishing. Contractions that have been induced with Pitocin come on suddenly and are like a massive, unannounced, unprepared squeeze, with no preamble and no slow fade.

They were super intense and super painful from the get-go.

They really hurt.

And, after a few hours, I was already getting tired and was silently crying with each contraction.

Now, Paul—who had seen his ex-wife through the birth of all three of their children—was surprisingly cavalier about the whole thing; that is, until he saw those tears rolling down my face.

He hated seeing me in physical pain like that.

It grated against every ounce of his training.

Paul was an anesthesiologist.

He kept encouraging me to get an epidural. I didn't want one. Not because I was afraid of the side effects or because I felt it was dangerous—I didn't want one because I wanted to be strong.

"I'm fine. I don't need any medication. Women have been doing this for centuries. I want to do this naturally. My sister has. I can too!" That was the reasoning I offered to him, and it was good enough for me.

And at first it really was fine.

I was fine.

I was finding ways to cope with the pain.

Paul was not.

He was trying to persuade me to get the medication and in the midst of his pleading, our conversation was cut short by one of the hardest contractions I had experienced.

I was squeezed around the middle and down through all of my tenderest places. It came out of nowhere and set in with an intensity that made me catch my breath. I was sitting on a big, bouncy sort of ball, and I doubled over in pain.

The red ball beneath me felt like a boulder and I looked over at Paul with pleading eyes through a tear-stained face.

He rubbed my back and once it stopped, he helped me with unusual tenderness to get into my bed.

He took a seat beside me, held my hand, looked me in the eyes. I was surprised. He was usually so clinical about the physical functioning of the body and while he was loving and caring, tenderness wasn't a common part of his repertoire.

Even when I was sick, he would just plunk a box of tissues and a trash can near my bed, tuck me in, turn off the lights and tell me to sleep. No sitting on the bed, stroking my hair, offering to rub my back. That was not his style—at all.

So this moment felt really meaningful to me.

All of that flashed in my brain as he sat there with me in my white gown with little blue flowers all over it, slowly recovering from that contraction. We were silent for a moment and then he asked me, "What is the primary job of the anesthesiologist during surgery?"

There it was!

The doctor was back in the house. The romantic, tender partner seemed to vanish.

The magic of the moment felt broken.

I looked at him with a combination of surprise and irritation. He had been so gentle and so loving and now he was quizzing me on medical data. I felt my heart sink a little inside of me. I had heard him explain the process of pain management many times before, and sitting beside me on a hospital chair while I recovered between contractions didn't seem to be the best moment for a pop quiz.

I made a face at him—our signature look that we called dog-face. He knew what I meant, and he proceeded without waiting for an answer. He told me that what they were really doing was blocking pain receptors, not knocking people out—another piece of information that I already knew.

"Why do you think they do that?" he queried again.

If he was going to put me through a stupid inquisition at this moment, I was determined to give him stupid answers and I replied quickly, "Well, it would be a bad thing if someone freaked out in the middle of surgery and jumped off the operating table, so there's that, I suppose."

My voice was snarky and my look none-too-pleased.

He was trying to be serious, and it was his turn to give me dog-face. He knew that I was annoyed with him, and he started to laugh.

"Yes, of course. Nobody wants that."

He had realized that I was taking his lecture poorly and made some sort of joke to break the tension. Between the funny dog-face he had made, and the laughter and the joke—combined with the fact that I had recovered from the last contraction fully by that time—my defenses were starting to soften.

He was trying to be helpful. I decided to really listen to what he was telling me and encouraged him to continue.

"When a body is in pain," he said, "the attention of the body is directed to the pain. The primary work that the body does, when in pain, is first and foremost the work to block the pain.

"It will do whatever it takes.

"The pain is the first thing it handles.

"The healing will not start until the pain stops."

I was watching the contours of his face as he spoke.

In that moment, I realized that this was him caring for me, not just as his girlfriend, but as the mother of his son, the baby that was working so hard to be born.

And he was so handsome, sitting there beside me, in his plain black tee shirt.

He had such a gift of breaking hard, complex medical issues into plain, simple explanations. I always loved and appreciated it, and this was no exception.

What he had just said was fascinating and that phrase emblazoned itself on my memory.

The healing will not start until the pain stops.

How often had I experienced the truth of that in my own life? And on this life-changing day, at this very moment, I had been given words to express it so simply, so clearly.

My heart was moved and the rest of his explanation about my body and when and how it would start to heal with and without the epidural only served to support the decision I made.

It was time to exit the pain.

I was happy to be convinced to change my somewhat loose birth plan and to order the epidural.

I gave birth to our beautiful, healthy little boy in the wee hours of the next morning.

Pain is something that I've never loved.

I'm a person who grows quite rapidly and with rapid growth, there is a lot of pain involved. When you stretch into parts of yourself you haven't explored before there is discomfort as you acclimate to that new space.

Just like when you exercise muscles that you haven't exercised before, soreness ensues, so too when you grow your own capacities be they emotional, intellectual or spiritual.

Because I love to grow and I embrace it, it often surprises me what my subconscious mind does to escape the pain and discomfort of the growth.

There was one time in early 2021 that I came face to face with my own escapism in a way that stopped me dead in my tracks and made me proceed quite differently.

I was on my weekly call with my business coach, walking along the side of a few parked cars, waiting to wrap up our call before I hopped on the elevator.

It had been an intense few months.

I had lost my dad six months prior and had taken a lot of time to grieve. For months and months, I had been focused on myself and my family more so than on my business. Of course, I was serving my clients and taking care of all of my obligations, but I hadn't been pushing myself or my business too hard. I had been gentle with myself, taking things slowly, enjoying the luxury of time and space to grieve, to rest, to recover from the crushing blow of losing my Dad.

My Dad had always been my person—the one I went to when things got tough or when things were joyful. He was my first call to celebrate big breakthroughs, my sounding board when I was working through gnarly issues. He got me. He loved me. He believed in me.

I needed him.

And he was gone. Suddenly and far too soon.

Heartbreaking barely describes it.

One of my friends, who had lost his dad a few years before I lost mine, told me that losing a parent is like losing a limb. You learn to live without it, to function without it, to adapt, but it never grows back. The pain stops over time as the wound heals, but every now and then you feel it again—that phantom limb pain—and you remember so vividly what you've lost.

I had been going through that process of recovery and had learned how to live without my dad. I didn't like it, but I had found firm footing and was beginning to genuinely smile again.

I had exited the most painful part and was starting to heal.

With my personal ship sailing upright again, I had begun to turn my attention back to my business.

Now, my business had gone through a nearly-as-dramatic—though entirely different—type of loss a little less than a year prior to the moment I was walking and talking to my business coach.

The loss had happened when the pandemic struck.

I'll never forget the day the World Health Organization announced the pandemic. It was a Wednesday. I had just gotten back from an international speaking engagement and was in the final stages of negotiating a few big corporate contracts. Just a few months prior, I had decided to focus my energy in my business on fewer clients but larger contracts. I had stepped away from working directly with the small business owners and had focused on large corporate clients. I had let my team go and had decided to keep my consulting business small and lucrative.

And it was working.

I had a few big clients lined up and, given the very specific nature of my work, the deals were done even though all the paperwork wasn't signed. We had verbal agreements, and the paperwork was just a formality. I had literally just pressed enter on my computer to submit the final piece of paperwork on the last of a few truly substantial contracts that would make this my best year ever.

I was sitting in my office, basking in the glow of success, feeling really excited about the months ahead. I was leaning back in my white chair, gently and oh-so-slightly rocking, with my hands behind my head, gazing at the ceiling, smiling from the tip of my toes to the curl of my lips. I was taking it all in. Soaking up the sheer enjoyment of having truly arrived.

I was so happy that I almost felt like I was floating on the rays of sunshine that were streaming in through the window.

I was reflecting on the journey to this point. It had been long and hard. When I first started my business, there had been days, weeks and months of struggle. Just three and a half years before I had been balled up, sobbing under my desk, snot running down my face, every piece of me feeling small and crushed. I was behind the locked door of my rented office space. I had bet big on an elaborate strategy that hadn't worked nearly as well as I had expected, and I was left almost penniless. That afternoon, sitting on that carpeted floor crying under my desk, I didn't even have money to buy diapers for my son.

It was devastating.

But I had taken a deep breath and gathered myself and leaned into the support that I had around me. Then, I made a plan and worked it and adjusted it and tried and tried and tried again until it started to work. I found my way. And, now, here I was, sitting in my office in my big, beautiful house in Scottsdale, Arizona, breathing a sigh of relief and joy. I had a little nest-egg and a business strategy that was finally, finally working consistently and delivering great results.

It had taken years and, in some ways, over a decade, but here I was. This was it.

I felt that I was finally, truly successful as an entrepreneur.

The projects I had lined up were exciting. The companies were amazing. The work was right in my sweet spot. Things were going to be great!

And then the announcement was made. Wednesday, March 11, 2020, the World Health Organization declared the pandemic.

In a matter of hours things became shaky and by Friday, when the president declared a national emergency, things in my business came to a slow and grinding halt. And, one by one, contract after contract got put on hold. Even projects that were agreed, signed, and ready to launch were indefinitely suspended.

Corporate clients froze their budgets.

Disaster plans were enacted.

Nobody knew what the future would hold, and everyone took drastic measures to survive.

By Monday morning I had lost nearly every single contract that I had. In five days, I lost hundreds of thousands of dollars of contracted revenue.

But I didn't panic.

I had enough working capital to weather a bit of a stormy season. I wasn't independently wealthy by any stretch of the imagination, and I certainly couldn't go forever without income, but I ran the numbers. I could make some sacrifices and cut some expenses, and be ok for a while. I knew it wasn't going to be fun, but it wasn't going to be business-ending either, so I took a deep breath and continued onwards.

It wasn't a totally safe and secure feeling, but at that moment in history everyone was holding their breath, and at least I knew that I would be ok.

And then, exactly one week later, the smallest of all the contracts, the very last one left, the tiniest last bit that was still in the queue, cancelled.

It was the straw that broke the camel's back.

I was crushed.

In one short phone call, I suddenly went from ok to not ok.

The amount was very small, and the number didn't really change my financial situation, but in losing that last thread, something in me snapped. And I started to grieve. I was suffering a loss and it was at that very moment that I could feel it in its full weight and gravity.

It was late in the morning the Wednesday after the pandemic was announced. And I couldn't have felt worse. As happy as I had been a week prior, I was equally deflated. I felt defeated. I had worked so hard for so many years to get my business to be strong and healthy and consistent and, in that moment, I felt the crushing weight of every lost dollar.

I had been on my own personal development and healing journey for years, so I could very clearly and very quickly see that I was in shock and grieving real losses in my business. So I gave myself permission not to be ok.

For the rest of that day, I didn't do any work. I didn't push through, I just sulked.

I allowed myself to feel bad and I didn't even try to look for the silver lining on the proverbial rain cloud. I just stood in the rain and railed at the skies. I didn't try to think of solutions. I just moped around the house, complained to my friends, and cried.

I sat on my pity pot.

I let myself feel all my feelings without any judgment or limitations for the whole, entire day. I didn't make them worse than what they were, but I didn't suppress them either.

But what I did was set a limit. I gave myself one day. One day to feel it all without trying to change a darn thing and then I promised myself that, the next day, I would pull my resources together, consider my options, make a plan, and rally.

And rally I did.

After my one day of unmitigated self-pity, I pulled myself together, I took a good hard look at the incredible assets I had—the content, the connections, the resilience, and the reputation—and I decided that I would go on a campaign of unmitigated generosity.

Every day on the news, there were stories of people getting sick, stories of death, of disrest, of businesses failing and families suffering. I knew that I had more than many and I wanted to do something good with it.

I made it my mission not to be outdone in generosity and to serve as many people, to help as many companies, as I possibly could during this moment of panic and uncertainty.

And I built a plan to do exactly that. I built out content that people needed in that moment and then I leveraged my corporate connections, my email list, my social networks, to get it out there as much as possible. And, in just six weeks, I helped 6,800 companies in my industry weather the beginning months of the pandemic and set themselves up for the success that ended up coming their way.

It was one of the best things I've ever done in my business, and the one that made me the least money.

Money isn't always the best or the most reliable measure of success.

Sometimes the things that we want to achieve, the mile markers we want to pass, don't work out and we have to let go of our attachment to our plan, we have to accept a new reality, and in doing that, we leave space for magic to happen.

My own businesses started to pick back up with smaller contracts. The big ones never did come back.

And, six months later when I lost my dad, I was grateful that those big, heavy obligations weren't on my plate after all and that I had the time to grieve his loss and to recover.

There is a Wisdom greater than us that guides us towards what we need even though it may mean that we have to relinquish our attachment to what we want in the meantime.

So, the afternoon when I was walking and talking to my business coach was a time when I had actually seen all of this already. It was far enough behind me to benefit by hindsight. I was well out of the painful part of it, had passed through enough of my grief to be able to start to heal and to have the emotional energy to start working on my business again.

During that conversation, I was feeling motivated and encouraged, but I was feeling a little stressed and anxious too.

I was telling my coach about my plans and was talking about the hurdles in my business. I had been listing thing after thing that would soon get better. I was talking about getting through this time of hard work to reach an easier point where growth wouldn't be quite as hard and quite as taxing.

She was listening closely, and when I stopped the flow of my stream of consciousness update on what I was working on and where I was trying to go, she sort of chuckled. It was the kind of chuckle that a parent makes when they see their little child doing something adorably sweet but not likely to get them to the outcome they want. The chuckle sounded just like their gentle indulgence over an innocent comedy of errors unfolding before them.

It was clear to me that she wasn't convinced of my plan.

And then she said with a consoling tone that almost sounded like pity, "Oh, Madeleine!"

Shoot.

I knew I was in for it when she said my name in that way.

My eyes took on a laser-like intensity as I continued to pace the floor.

"Hakuna Matata is a lie."

She said that statement and then was silent. So was I.

I wasn't expecting that, and it caught me off-guard. It took a minute for my mind to shift from my planning and future-vision thoughts to trying to puzzle out what she could mean by that statement.

"Hakuna Matata?" I thought to myself.

The only context I had for that phrase was the song from the Lion King. And I ruled it out almost instantly. Surely she can't possibly mean that, but the thought persisted and I hummed the words in my mind, "Hakuna Matata, it means no worries for the rest of your days… It's a problem-free philosophy! Hakuna Matata…"

No worries?

No worries. Yes! That was it. That is what she meant.

I was describing for her a future with no worries. I saw exactly what she was saying and what I had been doing and I froze.

Until that very moment I hadn't realized that I was chasing a mirage.

She let me process for a little while in silence and then continued to tell me that there is no such thing as life with no worries.

"You will always have worries," she said. "Best case scenario, you get to trade up your worries. You go from worrying about survival, to worrying about success, to worrying about making an impact.

"You go from wondering if you're going to have money for food and diapers, to wondering if your big clients are going to sign for six months or six years, for a thousand dollars or a million. After that you'll worry about how to achieve significance by doing good in the world around you.

"And, if you're doing it well, your worry stops being a massive preoccupation and becomes more of a joyful expectation."

It was a stunning reality and as she spoke, my brain caught up with my senses, and I blinked my eyes and looked at the world around me with a sense of relief.

You see, striving towards something that doesn't exist is taxing. You work and work and work to get to a destination, but the destination keeps changing because it isn't real. It isn't fixed. It isn't actually achievable.

When I realized that I had been planning to work towards a life with no worries, and I saw that wasn't a real option, the stress of it all instantly disappeared and I was able to recalibrate myself towards something more real, more concrete, truly doable.

There is an incredible gift in letting go of things that no longer serve us, in recognizing when we are working towards a false outcome, in seeing that what we are doing is not going to equal the result that we intended.

When we can see it, we are one step closer to being able to release our attachment to it, to let it go.

When we can release our grip on the thing that is actually hurting us more than helping us—like that electric fence from my crazy childhood games or the medicine-free birth plan I dreamt up—we can stem the negativity and find space in our life for something better.

And once we have let it go, if we are really brave, we can forgive ourselves for grabbing the darn wire in the first place.

THE INVENTORY
OF LETTING GO

♥

When you embrace growth, there will absolutely be things that you need to let go. The further inward you travel, the more you will need to let go.

Sometimes it's a piece of yourself. An old dream that isn't aligned with who you are or where you are in life, a habit that's been with you for years, a pattern of thought or speech or behavior that's no longer serving you.

Other times it's a relationship or a friendship or partnership.

Whatever it might be, the path of growth is paved with the stones of letting go.

And the most important things to let go of are the things that cause you pain. The unresolved traumas. The wounds and hurts that we all accumulate along the path of life. Those need to be released because you cannot heal and grow until you exit the pain.

Staying stuck in a painful situation or reliving the hurt of unresolved trauma will stunt your growth. You will remain in survival mode in the impacted area of your life no matter how much you want to thrive, no matter how strongly you feel the urge to soar.

So as a first step towards that thriving, soaring, up-leveled living, I want to encourage you to make an inventory of letting go.

Grab a piece of paper and get into a calm and quiet state. Take a few deep breaths. Find that inner sanctum—that place of psychological safety where it is good and safe to give voice to what you already know.

Take a few more deep breaths and let the list flow. Nothing is off limits to explore.

Once you are complete, you will have an inventory of letting go.

Read it over several times and ask yourself where you might be willing to start. Trust what jumps out and consider what small first step you might be ready to embrace.

It's amazing to see what your hands can hold when you have the courage to let go of what no longer fits.

♡ *Madeleine*

CHAPTER 9

START YOUR OWN TABLE

"Don't be afraid to give up the good
to go for the great."

— ROCKEFELLER

I'LL NEVER FORGET THE DAY THAT I INTERVIEWED FOR MY CORPORATE JOB.

I WAS THREE AND A HALF YEARS INTO my thriving career and had been flown up from Texas to New Jersey to meet with the executive leadership team one-on-one.

Their headquarters was a big, two-story building on the front side of a grassy field that, at this stage of the year, was yellowing in preparation for a long cold winter. The leaves on the trees were mostly gone. The glass facade of the entryway looked imposing and intimidating in the pale light of that late fall morning.

I had been feeling the bubbling up of exquisite jitters since the moment I had woken up. As I walked into the building, in my sleek black suit and tall, elegant heels, the feeling intensified. The two ladies at the front desk were kind but they looked like they had been in their roles forever and it was clear that they were highly experienced in the art of gatekeeping. They told me to sit, and someone would be down to get me in a few minutes. The small waiting area to the right of the entry felt pristine and a bit stiff. I didn't know if

I should sit there poised and patient, or casually leaf through the magazines on the table that so prominently featured their brand.

I had never worked for a company this big before.

They were the leading brand in our industry and their presence spanned the globe. I had always worked with emerging brands that were trying to rival them but would never be more than b-, c- or even d-players in the marketplace. Nobody could hold a candle to Somfy. It was exciting to have been pursued by them.

I had started a small, multi-line repping firm on my own nearly six months earlier. What that meant is this:

I had moved from Florida to Texas and, in the transition, I noticed that many of the companies in my industry that sold products throughout the eastern Gulf Coast didn't have anyone to represent their product lines to the small businesses who would buy them in the western Gulf Coast.

I saw the opportunity and figured out a way to fill the void.

I quickly went about the process of analyzing and selecting the products I knew I could sell effectively and the brands that would complement each other easily. Then I approached the owners of those companies, and worked out deals with them to be their independent product representative in the territory I identified as mine.

I figured out that, because nobody else was doing it, we could sell their product lines for a little bit more than what they did on the eastern Gulf Coast, and that the additional profit would more than cover the fees I proposed as my compensation.

It was a win-win all around.

The market was ripe, and I was eager and hungry.

Everybody I approached said yes.

And, voilà. My very first business was born.

It was a sweet gig perfectly tailored to my strengths and experience. And I made it work.

I made it work so effectively that I had started to erode Somfy's market share in the territory where I focused my efforts.

Somfy took notice.

At first, I had only won the business of some smaller companies here and there, but when I started to approach their largest, most valuable customers they went from noticing me to trying to recruit me.

The first time someone from Somfy had called me for a potential position, they offered me an entry level job that was 50% of the salary I was making working for myself. I turned that down, hard. I told them to come back to me when they had something a little more serious to offer me.

I remember the manager who first called me was initially surprised that I wasn't fawning over an opportunity to work with a market leader. I told him how much work I had put into developing my market knowledge, product knowledge, and my customer base. I wouldn't dream of leaving all of that for a step-down, no matter how big and well-regarded the brand.

Prior to our call, he had judged me based on my age and had allowed that number to create a perception of me as far less accomplished than I actually was. And, by the end of our call, he had a clearer picture of my experience and understood why the role he had offered wasn't a good fit. We parted on friendly terms.

He told me they would be back in touch.

It took several months, but they did eventually call again to suggest a role that felt far more commensurate with my experience and my salary expectations.

At first, I wasn't really sure if I wanted to give up my own business to pursue the opportunity, but I decided to embrace the process with gusto, so that I could discern whether this might be the next best move for me.

I put my best foot forward and the initial interviews had gone well enough that they wanted to meet me in person. By the time they offered to fly me up to the corporate headquarters, I had given it serious thought and consideration, and had decided that I really wanted to land this opportunity.

I showed up at their corporate headquarters that morning and performed at my absolute best.

The time whizzed by. It was far more exciting than intimidating, and as the day wore on, it had become very clear there was a mutually good fit between us.

It was time for my last interview.

The interview with the CEO.

His assistant popped into the office where I was waiting to let me know that he was ready. She walked me down the hall to his big, beautifully-appointed corner office. Michael had been at the helm of the North American division of the business practically since its inception and he was a legend in our industry.

As I walked in, I noticed that his office was full of pictures of him with all sorts of industry leaders, with awards, recognitions and even trophies. It was clear he was proud of all that he and the company he led had accomplished, and rightly so. Despite all that grandeur and the big imposing desk he occupied, he was super approachable and made me feel very welcome. He walked over to my side of the desk to greet me.

He had already heard good things about me. I had impressed all the right people throughout the day and this conversation was more about ensuring this was a good fit than putting me through the ringer. I could feel it and he told me as much.

We chatted about the company and its market-leading position. We talked about the French parent company (I casually mentioned my French language skills) and how they impacted the North American division, his division. We talked about the role and what it would take to get the territory I was inheriting to a good place.

We discussed his leadership style and the management team I would be working under, and then we started to talk about me and what made this a good fit for me from my perspective. We talked about my experience and my success. We went over the structure and process of building out the little business I had started. We talked about what I would have to do to transfer my business to another person or to shut it down, and we discussed a timeline for how long that might take.

He was anxious for me to get going in their company and he started to test me a little bit on my willingness to give up my entrepreneurial freedom. He dwelt on the drawbacks of the job, the fact that I would have to be held accountable to their processes and metrics and management structures. He brought up the difficulties I would face taking over a neglected and unmanaged territory, how I would have to go into some of my current customers and unsell them on the products I just sold them. He talked about how slow growth would be compared to what I had just built.

He was masterfully unselling me on the role to see just how serious I really was.

And that's when I looked him directly in the eyes and said, "None of that is going to be a problem. I have a plan. I have things lined up to make this work. I can handle it.

"Look, I'm only considering taking this job because I want to climb the corporate ladder."

He looked at me with an expression that was 30% surprised, 30% impressed, 30% curious and 1% offended.

I didn't waiver.

I doubled down.

"I don't want you to hire me," I continued, "if there isn't going to be room to promote me within the next two years. If there isn't any hope or space for me to be promoted up here, to the corporate office, I would rather keep doing what I'm doing.

"The money is the same, so that's a lateral move for me unless there's room to grow.

"I love the idea of working with an A-brand, a market leader, so well-funded and well-positioned, but all of that is secondary.

"I'm ambitious and I want to be sure that there's room to grow here if I'm going to step away from a business that is 100% mine and that's already showing signs of being very successful."

The eye contact was uninterrupted.

He flashed a big smile at me and then he got serious.

"You'll have to earn it," he replied.

"I wouldn't have it any other way! I'm ready to prove to you that I'll be worth promoting."

The eye contact continued, and a pregnant silence hung in the air.

One second elapsed, then two, then three. I could feel the momentum of a decision moving in his mind.

I sat there still and poised with my hands resting in my lap, my eyes soft but strong, my breath gently rising and falling in my chest. I wasn't moving, I wasn't speaking, but I was doing something incredibly important—I was holding space for his decision. The silence was rich and full.

Silence is not doing nothing.

"Deal."

That one word broke the silence and let the joy of the moment pour out. The decision had been made. We both felt euphoric. It was a win-win and he stood up from his desk, walked over to me, with his hand extended for a handshake. As I stood up and shook his hand, he said, "Welcome to Somfy!" He clasped me on the shoulder and walked me to the door of his office.

I've told this story many times and I've often been asked how I could be so bold. People think it's just how I am as a person, and they often believe that they couldn't do likewise. While my personality does play a part, the thing that truly fueled my gumption was a crystal-clear understanding of exactly what I wanted.

When I had decided that I wanted the role at Somfy, I thought about my future, and where I wanted to take my life. I hadn't grown up seeing myself as a successful entrepreneur, or as a highly respected executive leader. I had grown up in a blue-collar family with a couple of examples of strong females succeeding in their careers, but I hadn't dreamt of replicating their success because I didn't feel drawn to their fields.

But, as I had discovered the world of home improvement and all of the large and small businesses related to it, I had found my place and inspiration. The more I worked for people who recognized and rewarded and called out my potential, the more I had seen it for myself. The more I had surrounded myself by highly successful individuals, the more I recognized myself as one of their peers.

And, in being approached by Somfy, I recognized that a door had been opened to me to pursue success at a corporate level, and I knew that's what I wanted to do.

I didn't talk with Michael about wanting to climb the corporate ladder as some vague hope. It was my direct intention, and my actions and words were in powerful alignment with it.

I was unshakably sure I wanted to do it and I was unshakably sure that I could.

Most people wait to take action until they feel confident, but confidence comes second.

Courage comes first.

Confidence is the byproduct of successful outcomes. And it takes courage to leap into an activity or to take an action that has an uncertain outcome. I could be confident because I had already been successful starting something from the ground up—several times over. I knew I could do this. I had had successful outcomes that were similar enough to borrow from. I knew I was capable. And there wasn't a bad outcome either way. If he said no or if he was upset with me for being so bold and straightforward, I still had a great business I could continue to operate. If he said yes or if he was impressed, it was all upside for me.

It may look like I was lucky.

But luck isn't lucky.

Even in the luckiest of lucky cases, like winning the lottery, luck is still not strictly lucky. You have to decide you want to play, you have to get the tickets and then and only then is it possible that your number can be called. Without the ticket, there's no possibility of the win.

Luck happens at the intersection of preparation and opportunity—if and only if you act.

Preparation starts with belief. If we want something enough to act in its direction, there is an underlying belief that we can and will get it.

Belief is an essential component of preparation, and it takes courage to believe that you can get something that you've never gotten before or go somewhere that you've never gone before.

Let's imagine that you are single, never married, and you want to be married. In order to marry someone, you have to date and get to know them and build a relationship. You have to put yourself out there to get that first date. Unless you're working with someone who is going to arrange a marriage for you, there is no other way.

You have to date.

Walking in the direction of marriage starts with being ready and willing to date. If you are hurt and broken from past relationships, you have to heal those hurts and be ready to try again. That is part of preparation. You cannot get married if you don't take steps in that direction.

Preparation is the process of knowing what you want and then courageously removing all of the barriers standing between where you are now and where you want to be until confidence starts to build.

Then comes opportunity.

Remember, our brains are designed to seek proof of what we know, what we believe. When we know what we want and believe we can have it and have confidence moving in its general direction, the universe conspires to help us get lucky by putting us on high alert for those opportunities.

Opportunities, lucky breaks, don't always look so lucky or so special when they are happening. Sometimes they look accidental or are shrouded in a moment of doubt or disappointment. Other times they feel like the next logical step or an almost missed connection.

The mundane nature of opportunities makes many people miss them.

When I started working for Somfy, I made the decision that I would give my career five full years of intense focus. I wanted to climb that corporate ladder and I knew it would entail sacrifice. I knew I would have to move away from friends, work long hours, travel, forgo fun now and then. I made the mental and emotional commitment to do that the second I shook Michael's hand.

But success didn't happen overnight. It took time for me to get into the groove of working for a big company, to wrap up my own business, and to start to make good strides in my territory. It wasn't a fast and pain-free process. I made some mistakes and missteps before things got smooth, and I had to bide my time.

There is a lot of waiting in success.

And waiting is not inaction. It's taking actions that seem small and plodding and that amount to very little movement, if any, without losing hope in or sight of where you're ultimately heading.

It's planting the seed and watering it faithfully even though you don't see evidence of the sprout. If you stop watering, the budding seed will die. You have to believe that the seed is germinating under the surface even when you can't see it yet.

There is power in the pause.

It allows you to continue the process of preparation even when it's in quiet and hidden ways while still staying alert for the opportunity to present itself.

In my ardent desire to climb the corporate ladder, opportunity struck one day while I was least expecting it.

I was at a company event.

Earlier in my career I had attended a lot of events with other companies and, in the past, my work obligations ended when the event ended for the day, but with Somfy, everyone was expected to go to dinner with colleagues. It was something I dreaded. I love deep and meaningful connections and I'm not always good at or comfortable doing the superficial chit-chat that's often involved in these sorts of dinners.

On this particular day, the whole sales organization was going to dinner together in a private event space. There were regional managers, like me, field service reps, like the role I rejected, and then the whole management teams for both groups, direct and indirect, all the way up to but excluding the CEO.

There were probably 40 of us in the group.

I was among the first big wave of people shuffling into the well-appointed space.

I stood by one of the chairs at one of the round tables and watched as everyone started to pick seats.

I was looking for the right spot to sit.

A table with all the fun, young, cool people started to form. It was a few tables away and I considered making a dash to join them but it would have been extremely awkward for two reasons. First off, the room was filling up fast. There were already other people filling in the space between their table and mine. I would have had to push past them to reach the fun table without a firm guarantee that there would still be a seat left for me.

Secondly, although the group was composed of people in their early to mid-twenties—my age as well—this particular group had all known each other for a long time. You could see how comfortable they were with each other. I was still new to the team and wasn't really part of their clique. I would have been able to join in on the fun, but I would've been standing on the outside of so many of their long-standing inside jokes.

Although it wasn't practical to join them, I watched with longing and mild disappointment as all of the spots at their table were filled.

It happened so fast. People were settling in so quickly.

As the tables filled, I wished I had sat with them.

There wasn't really anywhere else for me to go.

As I stood there, hovering near a chair at my big empty table with its perfect white table cloth draped all the way to the floor, a few people started to come and sit down at the other side of the table, across from where I was standing. They were the executives. First one and then another one and then another one. I was still standing there, with empty seats to my left and right as nearly the whole rest of the table filled in with guys far more advanced in their careers—both in age, experience and in rank—than me.

I was the odd one out.

I felt discomfort creep over me. I was stuck with the boring old guys.

As if the dinner wasn't already going to be uncomfortable enough, now this! I was inwardly getting resigned to what promised to be the world's most boring, stiff, uncomfortable dinner ever.

I made one final glance around the room to double check that this was where I had to stay for the evening. I saw that every other seat was filled, except mine and the two on either side of me. People had settled into their spots and the gentle hum of their friendly chatter filled the air.

I took a deep breath and accepted that this was my table for the evening.

I sat down.

On the outside I was smiling, on the inside, I was still adjusting to this situation.

As I slid my chair in to the table, one of the market managers, a kind man who had been with the company for a very long time and held a prestigious position, jokingly suggested that maybe I didn't want to sit with a bunch of boring old guys and suggested that I might have a better time over at the table with the younger crowd. He pointed to the exact table I had wanted to sit at. Although he had read my mind, he was discreetly suggesting that I relocate.

I wasn't about to do that. There was literally nowhere else for me to sit, and I could imagine myself carrying my place setting, balancing my cup on top of my plate like some version of Oliver Twist, dragging a chair to an already filled table because I got gently booted from the grownups' table.

Absolutely not.

In that moment something in me changed. I went from hesitant and doubting to unshakably certain.

This was my table.

I had started it and I decided I was going to make the most of it. His discreet suggestion had galvanized me. I found my courage, laughed off his comment and flashed him my brightest smile as I retorted with a little lighthearted sass, "I would actually rather stay. We won't be the boring table. Don't worry! I'll bring the fun!"

That seemed to do the trick. We all knew that this was going to be our table, these were going to be our dinner companions. Something about the finality in my voice left no room for doubt.

The mood elevated a bit and everyone started chatting with their immediate neighbors.

I sat there in good-natured silence. I didn't have any neighbors. I was still surrounded on the left and the right by empty chairs.

I picked up a piece of bread and was just going to rip into it when, out of nowhere, my boss's boss's boss came and stood behind the chair directly to my left. I almost dropped the bread.

He was a dry person with an intimidating, stern, measured approach and he was about to be my tablemate. I had already decided that I was going to make it a good dinner, so even this shocker couldn't deter my resolve.

I looked up at him, shrugged my shoulders, smiled and said with a laugh, "Well, come on in, I don't bite!"

All of my negative internal narrative from a few minutes prior had vanished. This did not have to be a tragedy. It could be a comedy.

And I was determined that it would be.

As he sat down, we were all sort of crunched together. The table was probably designed to fit eight comfortably, but there were nine seats and we were a bit squished. I had been in food service and catering throughout college and I knew that the extra chair next to me could be removed. I wanted it gone so that I could let go of that one remaining shred of discomfort. I didn't need a huge neon arrow pointing to the empty seat next to me, advertising the fact that nobody actually wanted to sit there.

I could fix that, remove the problem.

So I flagged down a server and asked him to clear away the extra setting to my right. I told him we needed to remove the chair, as well as the linens and setup, so that we could all have a little more breathing room.

It was done in a flash, and I encouraged everyone at the table to scootch their chairs and shuffle their place settings so we could all spread out a bit and get a little bit more comfortable.

I was happy to have the empty chair gone—that had been my primary motivation—and the extra space for everyone else was a nice bonus.

When everyone had shuffled and adjusted to the extra space, our table was instantly more pleasant.

I was the most junior at the table, by a long shot.

And I decided to be the ambassador of a good time. We laughed and joked throughout dinner. I had my boss's' boss's boss, let's call him John, on my left, doing silly games with coins like trying to pick up a quarter from flat off the table with a perfectly flat hand, no fingers. It was hilarious. He tried and tried and tried and could not do it. Then every other person at the table had to make a go of it. Everyone else did it after a few tries, not him. He was more lively than I had ever seen him before.

We had great wine—a bonus of being at the table with the executive leadership team—and really excellent conversation. I wasn't on my best behavior, I was at my most authentic, and when you shine as your full self, discomfort and all, you have a magnetism that no amount of professional polish can imitate.

That was definitely the case that evening and our table was by far the best that night—even better than the fun, young crowd.

Around dessert time John turned to me and said, "I'm really impressed with how you took charge of the seating at the beginning of dinner. You saw a need and you jumped in. It didn't matter that you were the least senior at the table, the only female. Well done!"

I smiled and said thanks and made some comment about it being no big deal.

He replied with, "Ok, so, ask me anything."

"Anything?"

"Yes. Anything."

I took a deep breath while my mind had a little, mini-internal struggle. I could ask him about his family or the early starting years of his career, or how he got to his high position. Or, maybe, just maybe, this was my golden opportunity.

Maybe I could ask him about that ladder I wanted to climb.

Our conversation had been lighthearted and fun, and it wasn't a super serious environment, but this was it. He was a shot-caller, a decision maker, and a leading executive.

This was my opportunity.

I was not going to waste it with a banal question.

I pivoted my body in my chair to devote all of my attention to him. I looked him square in the eye and I asked, "What is it going to take for me to be promoted up to corporate?"

I went from laughing and joking to dead serious over the course of that one deep breath.

He saw it and responded in kind.

I could tell he was surprised but took my question with as much seriousness as I had asked it. "Ok," he answered deliberately, "let's talk about that. There aren't any open roles right now, but that doesn't mean that there isn't space for you. What do you have to offer?"

Now we were cooking.

We chatted for a solid twenty minutes about my skills and my professional interests. We talked about things that the organization needed, the gaps and the walls. We discussed the market and our brand, our strengths and weaknesses. He told me to draft up a proposal of a strategic project that I might want to spearhead that aligned with something we had discussed, to send it to him with my resume and he would see what he could do.

Within four months I had been promoted and relocated to work at the corporate office.

Sometimes you have to start your own table.

You have to be courageous.

You have to not only accept but also embrace, with joy, those profoundly uncomfortable moments. You have to decide to get past the discomfort of a situation way outside of your comfort zone. You have to be willing to stretch to find commonality with people you may not perceive as your equals. You have to be ok with not having been wanted, invited, pursued, and hold your own anyway.

And it's in those very moments that magic sometimes happens, and you end up getting lucky, very intentionally lucky.

YOUR LUCK SCORE

———————————— ♥ ————————————

Early in my career, being called lucky used to offend me. It felt like (and maybe sometimes was) a cut down, a minimization of my effort, my work, and my sacrifices and an overstatement of the role of blind luck.

But as I grew across all the dimensions of myself, so did my perception of being lucky. I came to realize that luck isn't so blind or random afterall. In fact, in most cases it takes years, sometimes even decades of persistent effort to get to a place where luck can lift you forward.

I look back now with pride on being so lucky so early in my career.

And, just as success does, luck leaves clues.

The more aware we become of what it takes to get lucky, the luckier we can become. So, take a moment to calculate your own personal luck score and see if you're as ready to get lucky as you think!

♡ Madeleine

LUCK SCORE QUIZ

Read the following five statements. Give yourself from 1 to 20 points for each. The higher the points, the more fully the sentence applies to you, so 20 points is 100% alignment.

1. I am clear on where I am going in my life.
2. I consistently put myself out there regardless of the outcome.
3. I am on the lookout for opportunities, even in the unpleasant or mundane.
4. I am grateful for where I am now and what I have today.
5. I am open to change and fully prepared to take action.

Tally up your score. That, my friend, is your own Personal Luck Score.

If you're surprised by your score, don't worry!

Sometimes we are not ready for luck to strike because we don't know who we are or where we want to go. Maybe we're resentful of having to start at our current moment. Perhaps we are too comfortable in the known, the familiar, the routine to take the leap when the door cracks open. Whatever's holding you back, know that it's surmountable. Pick one statement and start there.

Remember, luck shows up in the inches, not the miles.

For more, check out www.madeleinemacrae.com/gifts

CHAPTER 10

TRUE NORTH

"When the inexpressible had to be expressed, Shakespeare laid down his pen and called for music. And if music should fail? Well, there was always silence to fall back on, for always, always and everywhere, the rest is silence."

— ALDOUS HUXLEY

MY SON'S DAD PASSED AWAY IN LATE 2021.

T HE DAY BEFORE HE DIED, Paul had been chatting with his son, sitting on FaceTime with us as we read bedtime stories. It was Noah's seventh birthday and Paul wanted to spend as much of the evening with him as possible. When it was time to turn off the lights and settle down to sleep, he had said his goodnights and sent all the hugs and kisses. He had asked me to call him back when Noah was sleeping.

Now, I usually had very clear boundaries with Paul.

We were co-parents, not friends.

Paul's life had been tragic since we parted ways. He lost his business and his livelihood and had been reduced to the humiliating situation of living back at home with his mother, in his fifties, unable to provide for himself or his children.

It was hard to watch and even harder for him to endure.

In the early stages of our co-parenting journey, I had to keep my distance simply to protect myself. Although our relationship had taken so much from me and had left me so shattered, I still loved Paul, still found him attractive, still wanted him to find his way to solid ground, and still felt pulled to help him do that.

When Paul and I first started dating, he was going through a lot, and I thought that I was helping him get through the rough patch to the other side of the difficulty. I was looking at his life through the lens of mine and, in my life, even the roughest of rough patches has led to solid ground on the other side. I have always sought the solid ground. In his life, however, he would sometimes go through a tiny lull but would end up in waters even darker and stormier and more dangerous. His life wasn't a navigation through, it was a navigation constantly further and deeper into turbulence.

I could only see that after I was out of the boat, so to speak, so I had to hold strong boundaries so that my compassion would not go haywire and compel me to jump back in. I had to keep my distance so that I would not be tempted to dive into the water to save him from the constant state of drowning in which he found himself.

I knew that jumping back in would lead to me being pulled under the water.

I had nearly drowned once, and I wasn't willing to risk it a second time.

From the day my coach told me the drowning person at the resort story, I had been very careful about my boundaries with Paul.

As time progressed, and my romantic feelings subsided, and I felt stronger and more capable of handling the splashing water, I would come closer and would let my guard down. Time and time again it led to aggravation, hurt and upset. It was too disruptive to be worth the risk, so I had to remain vigilant and to keep those boundaries really strong even when I hadn't wanted to, and even when it felt unnecessary.

Despite my need for strong boundaries, I always gave Paul full and unfettered access to my son—his son. From day one, I knew that Noah would want to love both his parents and that no long-term good and only long-term harm could come if I made him choose, if I spoke ill of his Dad, if I poisoned his heart. So I didn't do any of that. I put up strong boundaries for myself and I kept a watchful eye with our child, so all the storytime and the facetimes, the calls and the conversations that they wanted flowed often and freely. And in those interactions, I wasn't the primary interlocutor, Noah was.

My connection with Paul was friendly and cordial and sometimes even a bit chatty, but it wasn't deep, and it certainly didn't include private conversations after Noah was asleep.

But that night was different.

There was something different about Paul when he asked me to call him back. I couldn't articulate it, but I could feel it, so I promised him I would.

When the house was quiet and I could hear the soft, sleeping breaths that Noah was taking, I slipped out of his room, brewed myself a cup of steaming hot tea, settled into my favorite white glider, and called Paul back.

I was perched up in our apartment on the thirty-first floor, looking out over the twinkling lights of the city. The sky was a deep dark blue—not pitch black yet—and it was peaceful all around.

And our conversation was peaceful too.

We chatted about our son, his school year, how he was doing just a year after losing my dad—his beloved Papa. Paul had been a godsend when my Dad got sick. He was a walking medical resource center and broke down the test results for me and my family in plain English. His issues, our boundaries, all of it were set aside as he stepped into the role of counselor and medical interpreter—a role where he shone brightly. He told us what was good news and what was worrisome. He told us when things were probably worse than what we were being told by the hospital, and then he told me exactly what to ask, in strong medical terms, so that the doctors would take me seriously and tell me the unfiltered truth. And they did. He explained to us the disease process and helped us be as prepared as we could be for the end.

He was incredibly supportive and had really stepped up on taking advantage of his parenting time after Dad died too. In that one year, he had come to Phoenix for a week so I could get away for some much-needed time on my own to do some grieving and healing in private. He had taken Noah for Spring Break and then again for a few weeks during the summer. It was so nice. Nothing like that had happened in many years—not since Noah had been two years old.

Noah and I were both so happy.

And so was Paul. He adored his little boy and was delighted to have so much time with him.

There couldn't have been a better win-win-win.

As we were talking about Noah and his grief and how much better both Noah and I had been doing, I thanked Paul for all that he had done for me, for my family, just one year prior. I had thanked him many times before, but there was something special about the conversation that night.

There was no turbulence lingering in the air like there had often been. It just wasn't there.

He said that no thanks were needed. He told me that he loved me, and he would always be there for me whenever I needed him.

He didn't pause for an answer—he knew I would have told him that he would always have a special place in my heart as the father of my son but that I didn't love him in a romantic way and hadn't for many years.

He continued, "I know I've told you this before, but maybe I didn't say it all, so I wanted to tell you how sorry I am for what I did to you—not just at the end—but all of it. You deserved better. I hurt you and you were never anything but good to me. It was wrong. I was wrong. And I am so sorry."

I stopped rocking.

I deepened my gaze into the darkening sky. He had said some of that before, but there was more to his apology this time. Some level of understanding, some ownership of harm, and some genuine accountability that I had never heard before.

"Paul," I answered, "I forgave you a long time ago. You are forgiven. Truly, a hundred percent, forgiven."

I had told him that in the past, too, but even on my side there was a level of sincerity that had never been there before. Of course I had meant it fully in the past and hadn't harbored anything ill towards him but, again, there was something different in the air this time. Often his apologies would be laced with a butterfly net—to see if maybe just maybe I was open to rekindling something between us or to snatch-out a drip of my pity or compassion. There was no net today at all. Nothing like that.

But something else seemed to be hanging in the air.

I usually kept these sorts of conversations, when they had happened in the past, as superficial as possible because I didn't want to invite emotional intimacy or to welcome a storm-surge of grievances that he had with the world at large. It didn't feel like a flurry of self-pity or raging against the machine was imminent. The mood was much more pensive and there was something full about the pauses.

A deep and meaningful silence hung in the air. He was letting those words soak in as I was pondering within myself whether to take the conversation deeper than I usually would or just to wrap it up there and say my goodnights.

He broke the silence with, "I'm not so sure I deserve it."

I had my answer.

This was the moment to go deeper than I had before.

"Everyone deserves forgiveness, Paul. Everyone. There is nothing so heinous that you could do, that you could ever have done, that would be outside the scope of forgiveness. God is the one who forgives; and what's outside of the scope of God? By His very nature, God is omnipotent and if one single human could do anything that was outside of the scope of forgiveness, God would be no more.

"You aren't bigger than God. Your transgressions—no matter what they have been, no matter what—are not bigger than God.

"Nothing that you have done or that you could have done is outside of the scope of forgiveness.

"If I have forgiven you, and God is willing to forgive you, what is holding you back from forgiving yourself?"

"I've deserved everything that I have gotten. I left a wake of hurt behind me for so long," he answered, with a level of compassion and of personal ownership of his role in that hurt that I hadn't ever heard from him before.

And I followed up with, "And don't you think you've paid for it long enough? How long are you going to have to suffer until you think you've suffered enough? What is it going to take to clear you?

"You have already suffered enough.

"You do not have to continue to suffer.

"You are suffering by choice now.

"What if you didn't have to? What if you made a different choice? You certainly can. Nobody expects you to continue like this. You can make a new choice. You can do it. You can decide to just ask for forgiveness and to be forgiven and it can be done.

"Are you ready, really ready, to be forgiven?"

A rich silence hung in the air between us. The evening sky had intensified from the deep blue of late evening into a rich, dark, inky black of night. The nighttime-covered city sparkled outside of my window like a blanket. Nurturing, strong, protective.

With hesitance in his voice, he finally spoke.

"I think I might be."

Another moment of pregnant pause.

"I really think I might," he concluded, with more certainty in his tone than his words conveyed.

And that was the first time I had ever—in the decade I had known him—heard it in his voice: hope.

Genuine hope.

I sat back in my chair and began to gently glide again. I kept looking out the window at the twinkling lights of the city and I urged him to talk to God, to ask for forgiveness and to let the gift of forgiveness flow into his heart. To let him forgive himself.

I told him, "There is something almost magical that happens when we embrace forgiveness.

"When we forgive, it is not the other who is healed, it is us.

"And when we are both the forgiven and the forgiver, the impact is compounded exponentially.

"That's why it's so hard to do—because we not only have to offer the olive branch, we have to accept it at the same time too.

"You can do this.

"I did it.

"And if I can, you can. You are so strong and resilient and ready.

"Paul, you are so so ready.

"You deserve it. Imagine the peace it will bring your soul."

My words were gentle, strong, and inviting. They flowed effortlessly as I spoke about the riches of forgiveness and urged him to translate his hope into action and to turn the page of this chapter of such extreme sadness and suffering.

Our conversation ended with a level of peace I had never felt for him or with him ever before.

It ended with boundless hope and deep peace.

He unexpectedly died in his sleep the very next night.

That was my final conversation with Paul and it closed out our sometimes-tumultuous relationship with the Theological Virtues—the three-fold blessings of Faith, Hope and Love.

And what a gift that was.

Being able to talk about how their dad died with the children he left behind and to point towards the light of Love, the wellspring of Hope, and the pivot towards Faith was a mercy unlike any other that I had ever experienced. Any consolation for their broken hearts was meaningful to me and to them, and this one, in particular, carried a profound balm.

Paul always loved his kids very deeply and, when he could, expressed that love by lavishing them with gifts. It was just his style to leave us all with such a big, important gift. Our final earthly conversation has been a spring to which I have traveled many times, and from which I've often drawn a deep draught of solace.

I'll be forever grateful for that conversation. Seeing the door of hope open like that on the threshold of eternity delivered a level of closure and of peace to me that may not have been available to me in any other way.

It was a tremendous gift that came under heartbreaking circumstances, wrapped in such hard to accept wrapping paper.

I'll always imagine Paul cradled in the hands of hope, surrounded with everlasting peace.

Rest easy, my friend!

Death comes for all of us.

It is inevitable.

No matter when or how or why, it will mark the end of our earthly sojourn and if we are oriented in the direction of success or of wealth or of pleasure or of riches or of anything as ephemeral as that, we may miss the true north: peace.

Peace is the right-ordering of our lives with our souls.

It is the hidden conversation between our conscience and our actions and when either side of the conversation is out of balance, we cannot find peace. We will not find peace.

Peace is a compass that always points inward and upward.

Happiness is a compass that always points outward.

And it's a tricky one. Chasing happiness, wanting to be happy, seems like it's the right thing, the best way to navigate, but it's not.

Peace is.

When Noah was just a little shy of four years old, he happened upon the old animated TV show, "Transformers". He had always loved vehicles and had seen a few cool robots that he liked too, so seeing vehicles that could transform into robots fascinated him in every way. He started to get obsessed with Transformers. He loved the animated shows, old and new, and as he got older, he loved the live action ones just as much.

He also loved the transforming figures—and not just the sim-plistic, age-appropriate ones that could flip into position in just a few easy moves. He loved the complicated, realistic ones which took twelve or fifteen moves to transform and mimicked the characters in the shows precisely.

Something about the intricacy of the mechanics captivated his imagination.

As soon as he realized that I was willing to buy him these incred-ible toys (he shared the gift-giving love language with his dad), he would talk me into going to the stores to look at them and to get for him the coolest one he discovered.

He loved these trips to the store. The vintage comic book stores, the mega-modern superstores, or even the small, superhero-ori-ented toy stores, he loved them all and would browse their selections in great detail. He would scour every single option from the front, back, sides. He would look at the designs and the features. He would line up his favorites and weigh them against each other painstak-ingly recounting the strengths and weaknesses, pros and cons of each character and each design.

At first, these store visits were fairly frequent, and we went from browsing and admiring to buying and acquiring—sometimes more than one at a time.

In an effort to prevent myself from becoming wildly over-indul-gent with my son, I weaned him off of the weekly trek to the nearest collectables or superstore and I made a trip to the Transformer aisle a special, occasional surprise or an earned reward with a very clear boundary of one toy within a specific budget range.

I figured that, with it now being a rarity, getting a Transformer would be a huge source of delight and would fill up his love-tank for a good long while. Considering that gift-giving was a primary love language for him, I thought that it would make him happy and feel content for a few days or even a week or more.

I was wrong.

It had the opposite effect than the one I intended.

The drive back from the store to the house was a very joyful one and for quite a few hours, while he mastered the transformations and looked over every millimeter of the design and the packaging—instructions and all—he would love and treasure, be satisfied with and totally engrossed in, that new toy.

But it didn't last.

It faded quickly, sometimes even before nightfall.

Time after time, the very next morning, before breakfast had even hit the table, he would start asking for another Transformer. Going to the store and seeing all of the newest and best inventory laid out before him, his just but for the asking, made him want all those toys or at least a few special treasures.

It stoked in him the consuming fire of desire and he would obsessively compare what he had to what he could have had.

There is an old adage that comparison is the thief of joy. And it certainly stole his from him.

His wanting more would rob him of his joy in having what he had.

Contentment—not complacency—is a skill and a gift that he had to gain mastery of far sooner in his life than he would have desired.

He was navigating towards happiness but it was leading him astray, as it does so many of us, because happiness is only found when we achieve what we have wanted, when we get what we expected, when our needs have been met.

Happiness is a byproduct.

It is a byproduct of the achievement, the getting, the fulfilling of our needs, desires, wishes. If your desire is for happiness, if you're navigating towards happiness, you're going to be stuck in an endless and an ever-more-voracious cycle of chasing, getting, and then redefining and chasing again, because the joy of the acquisition is a fleeting feeling that will have to be continually renewed.

If you map out your life to pursue something that isn't enduring and that can and does change with circumstances, you are going to be rushing around here and there and everywhere with a sharp feeling of lack, getting more and more frustrated that you can't get and hold onto the very thing you've poured yourself into chasing: happiness.

People are spending their whole lives chasing happiness and are only finding something ephemeral. There has to be a better way.

The better way is to pursue peace.

To seek it relentlessly.

When you pursue peace, you are forced to reconcile within yourself, to square up with the Lightning Rod Moments, to seek support, to heal, to forgive much—most of all yourself.

It may seem soft or fluffy or an easy, trite thing, but it is none of that.

Seeking peace requires much of us.

Seeing peace requires courage.

Seeing peace requires patience.

Seeking peace requires tenacious persistence.

It requires letting go.

It requires embracing forgiveness.

It requires holding onto the vision of where you are going without getting overly attached to the plan of how you're getting there.

And none of that is fluffy or frou-frou or easy.

Nor is it the work of one day or one week or even of one year.

It is the work of a lifetime. The iterative journey of the tenacious pursuit of peace through whatever doors life opens for you, Lightning Rod Moments and all, is not a simple, straight-forward path. It's full of twists and turns and unexpected routes. As we decide to get off of the repetitive looping track and go for the ascent, it can be harder and more daunting than we could imagine.

As I embarked upon my intensive inner healing journey in 2016, I didn't realize that I was seeking peace. I didn't know that I was doing something courageous. I looked back at my relationship with Paul and saw the woundedness of his heart, of his soul, and had recognized in myself wounds that drew him to me, me to him—and I resolved to discover, to understand, and to heal those wounds. Once and for all.

I had no idea it would take me so many years.

No idea how intensive it would be.

No idea how much it would change me.

And I'm glad I didn't know.

My dad used to say that if a mason saw all of the bricks that he would lay in his lifetime, he might very well never lift that first brick. That would have been me, the mason intimidated by the mountain of bricks. Had I seen the layers and had I known how relentlessly I would seek that healing, over the course of therapies and healings and coaches and guides and therapists of all disciples and types, I may have hesitated.

I may have withdrawn.

My determination may have been quenched by fear and I would have missed out on so much.

When things seem like they are going to be hard and scary and deep, it's easy to feel intimidated, to want to wait until you feel the confidence to act, have some assurance of success, see the simplification of the path; but if we wait for all that, we will spend our lives waiting.

It is a great gift to us not to know what the future holds in a sure and certain way.

I'm incredibly grateful that I decided so firmly, set my intention so unshakably, and acted when I had the courage to do it. I thought it would take me a few therapy sessions, maybe a little support here and there, but it was so much more than that.

Many years ago, toward the peak of my corporate career, I had started to see a therapist to work through some of my doubts and fears about relationships. It was 2011 and I had decided that I wanted to be in a marriage-minded relationship and to become a mom. I was nearing the end of my twenties and wanted to be on that family-building trajectory into my thirties.

I hadn't seen a therapist since 2008 when I had addressed my trauma the first time.

This was my second session with her. She was trained in the same therapeutic practices as my first therapist but came at it a little differently. She was far younger than my first therapist—closer to my age—and I really appreciated her style and approach. She was all about experiential awareness and would use vivid imagery and exercises to create moments of resonating insight.

I had looked her up and wanted her help, but I was complaining about having to be in therapy again. It felt strange to me and I said, "I already worked through my trauma. How come I have to do it again? Shouldn't I be better already?"

She looked at me with patient understanding.

She knew that we humans have all sorts of layers of trauma—both big and small—that have impacted the way that we see and interpret the world around us. She knew, although I didn't yet, that we can only address what we are ready to address as much as we are ready.

I once heard Oprah, quoting Matt Kahn, express it like this: "People can only meet you as deeply as they've met themselves."

And at that time of my life, I hadn't plumbed the depths of my own soul yet, so I didn't know how much could be available to me.

She was used to this.

And as I stared at her, expectantly, she explained.

"Imagine yourself as a big, old house. Strong and sturdy, with lots of rooms over two or even three floors. You start your life off empty and as things happen in and around us, we fill up those spaces, those rooms, with memories. Big things [what I now call Lighting Rod Moments] may fill out an entire room to the brim and keep you from going in there. Smaller things clutter up some of the spaces and we learn to navigate in and around our things—our baggage, if you will.

"When you addressed the big trauma in therapy the last time, you cleared out a whole bunch of space and that gave you the relief you were looking to find.

"And now you have grown, your awareness has increased, and you need more space.

"The more self-aware you become, the less and less clutter you can tolerate in your inner castle.

"When things happen that trigger you, you are being told that there is more to heal, more to resolve. Doing your first round of therapy—especially for a significant trauma—is like clearing out the room, but sometimes there is more inside of the closet of that room. It doesn't mean that the trauma wasn't resolved before, it means that you want more space, and that little, leftover clutter in the closet isn't tolerable for you anymore.

"When you are content to be hemmed in with your hoard of unresolved, unexamined incidents and issues and traumas, you're living in just one small room of your big huge inner home. You don't worry about all of the stuff crammed everywhere. You don't even see it. You just acclimate. You make pathways around the junk.

"But when you start to see that the things surrounding you aren't helping you, it's like you realize that you need more space, that you want to inhabit more of those rooms, to be able to move effortlessly, to truly live.

"And once you've cleaned out the living space and the closets and the cupboards, you will find that there comes a time when you can't even stand the dust bunnies in the corners anymore."

As she spoke, my stiff and uncomfortable posture relaxed a little. The intensity of my gaze softened. I leaned back into the chair and felt the curve of the supple leather supporting my back. I became aware of the comfortable warmth of the room.

I had imagined my own inner castle as she spoke.

I saw myself in a progression. First, I was living in a hoarded space. Dark, dirty, uninviting. And then I imagined the stuff being removed, the floors washed, the walls painted. I saw myself living in a crisp, clean, bright, welcoming environment—the type of home that I loved to have.

What she said struck me—not in a hard and harsh way—but in a gentle progressive way.

An understanding opened to me as she spoke.

And I could foresee a future where I was going over to a lovely empty closet, just off of my immaculately clean kitchen with white marble countertops. I saw myself reaching for the handle of a white door, opening it, looking down at the warm wooden floor and reaching in with my broom to whisk away a fluffy, gray dust bunny that had hardly even settled into place.

That felt like a place I wanted to live.

I didn't know it at the time, but I was building a future vision of my own interior dwelling—one ideally matched to where I was going and who I was becoming.

It took me well over a decade to create that space.

For many years, I functioned under the false belief that I would find inner peace when I was as successful as I had once set out to become, both financially and positionally. But with each milestone, I would see that I could do or be or have more. Every time I got close to the achievement, the goal line would move.

I remember my dad telling me once that he was listening to an interview of a successful business man whom he greatly admired. The successful entrepreneur had been asked what it felt like to be at the top. And his answer always stayed with me. He said that it was an empty bag.

Immense wealth.

Fame.

Success.

All of it is an empty bag.

Because success is not enough.

It never is.

It never has been.

We are made for more. We want more. We seek more.

The more deeply I have journeyed inward, the more I have found myself drawn upwards, drawn to look towards the heavens, towards the divine, towards God.

When I've externalized my search for happiness, for meaning, for success, I've floundered far more often than I've flourished.

When I turn the eyes of my mind inward, when I slow down and give myself space to sit in quiet contemplation, quiet conversation, I find intimacy. Divine intimacy.

When I cracked the cover of the first book that drew my attention to the possibility that my strengths were more important than my failings, when I made the decision to confront my traumas through therapy, when I embarked upon the intensive journey of healing my broken heart and broken spirit — a deep spiritual life wasn't what I was looking for. It wasn't what I wanted to find. It wasn't my intention.

I was looking for healing, for freedom from the pain, for wholeness. And the more I searched, the more I found that the restlessness I was looking to avoid and evade was the very thing that was calling me to go deeper.

In junior high I memorized a poem in poetry class, "The Pulley", by George Herbert. It tells the story of God letting every good thing flow upon mankind. God is narrating the event and he makes his way through all of the incredible things: beauty, wisdom, honor, power, strength, and as he approaches the very bottom of his glass of blessings, he pauses, seeing that Rest is the final gift at the bottom of the glass.

Before he pours out this one final blessing, he holds back his hand and decides not to give the blessing of Rest. He says this final stanza:
"Yet let him keep the rest,
But keep them with repining restlessness.
Let him be rich and weary, that at least,
If goodness lead him not, yet weariness
May toss him to my breast."

When things have gotten tumultuous in my life, when I have felt the depths of restlessness pulling at the strings of my heart, I have often remembered those words, and heard in them a call to go deeper, to search for meaning, to find the gift hiding behind even the ugliest wrapping paper.

But I never really considered what I might find when I looked. I never paused to factor in the possibility of finding peace. And I could never have imagined what finding peacefulness could yield. It has been beautiful beyond measure. Immensely satisfying. Incredibly fruitful.

Not so long ago I was chatting with one of my coaches. I was telling her how far away I was, financially, from where I wanted to be. I was hardly comfortable and far from what I perceived as truly wealthy. She responded very strongly to that statement, told me never to say that again, and then said something jaw-dropping to me. She told me, "Madeleine, you are wealthy in all the things that matter."

It struck me to the core.

It was a blinding flash of the obvious—an entirely new way for me to think about wealth and success. Never had I, in all of my nearly 40 years, ever considered that wealth could be something beyond money. And I pondered it for many weeks, added it to my vision board, and reminded myself of it daily.

What if success were measured by peacefulness?

What if wealth were measured in every and any thing except money?

How successful and wealthy could we all be and become if we shifted the narrative, if we adjusted the paradigm?

Material wealth and financial success are beautiful, but how much more enduring are those inner treasures?!

Go inward to go upward.

Embrace the ascent.

Taking the path of healing and of self-knowledge and of discovery and then learning how to deploy all of those things in the service of something more, of something greater, isn't the easy path. And its rewards are beyond what can be contained in a bank account.

When success is not enough, you must look within and seek a more enduring anchor.

And my wish for you is that you will not only tenaciously and persistently pursue it, but that you will also find it.

Luxuriate in it.

Dwell in it.

Abide in it.

Peace.

Deep peace.

Deep abiding peace.

EPILOGUE

MY TOES.

M Y TOES WERE NESTLED into the deep plush carpet beneath my desk.

The soft comfort of my feet stood in stark contrast to the tension in my shoulders, the upset in my stomach, the turmoil in my mind. I was worried.

I was deeply worried that the life I had worked so hard to put back together, piece by piece, after my breakup with Paul, would come crashing down around me.

I felt fragile.

I felt like anything more than a gentle breeze would bowl me right over and that all of my personal work and healing and effort, all of the time I had poured into regaining my financial footing, into building up a successful business, into relaunching my life as a single solo parent would be for naught.

And, if that happened, I felt like I wouldn't have the strength to pick the pieces back up again.

Nothing bad was happening in my life. In fact, my son and I had been doing so well that we had moved out of the sheltering comfort of my parent's home and had established ourselves in a beautiful new place that felt perfectly aligned with who I was and where I was in my life. It was as though I had been able to pick up the threads of my life from before my relationship with Paul and just start weaving anew without an interruption but with so much more wisdom and patience and peace.

But I couldn't seem to stop myself from thinking about the what-ifs. From worrying about things that might happen. I made up outlandish scenarios of loss like the sudden burning down of our home or a devastating injury or a debilitating illness. I knew it wasn't healthy and I also knew I did not want to repeat any of my past mistakes, so I reached out for some help.

The year prior, I had been in a mastermind group with a lady who practiced Feng Shui and she had talked about how transforming your space could help you achieve harmony. That was what I wanted. Harmony. Peace. Freedom from worry.

So I did a little searching and found a local practitioner I felt I could trust. I immediately booked an appointment and, just a few days later, we were on the phone together.

I told her about myself and said that I wanted her to come to my home, to show me how to fix the gaps energetically and how to set it up so that I would be optimally poised to succeed. She shared with me how she believed that we pick our homes for a reason. That they have something to teach us, something to give us and that, unlike other Feng Shui practitioners, she didn't believe in *fixing* a space. If there are holes in places where there shouldn't be, she felt they were there for a reason. She had heard my history and knew that I moved often and was even more convinced that optimizing my space was going to be more effective than trying to fix it.

I was mildly disappointed, but felt it was worth it to have her come to my home anyway. And I'm glad I did because our in-person meeting was super helpful. I learned to pay attention to the places

I would be walking by and looking at most frequently and to honor my bedroom as a sacred space.

"What we see when we first wake up and what we look at in the last moments before we sleep deeply impact our sleeping hours and our waking hours," she said. It resonated deeply and I made my room a beautiful refuge.

I felt great about what we had done together, and I loved the way my place looked and felt.

But after our work together, I had gone back to worrying about losing everything again. I still felt really unsteady so I had reached back out for a follow-up consultation.

I was sitting at my desk awaiting her call and my toes were sinking into the carpet. She wasn't only a Feng Shui expert, she was a Human Design practitioner too and I hoped that her familiarity with my chart would help me solve this problem.

The phone rang.

"This is Madeleine," I answered.

"Madeleine! Lovely to hear from you again. How can I help?"

My worries spilled out of my mouth almost faster than I could think. I told her how anxious I was, how worried I was that if something big went wrong in my life that I would be broken into a million pieces and wouldn't be able to put myself back together again. I told her I needed her to help me insulate myself, protect myself, prevent myself from making any missteps that could lead to that sort of a crash.

She listened, quietly, as I poured my heart out.

When I was done, she was silent for a moment and then said, "Well, Madeleine, that isn't going to happen. You are perfectly designed to crash. Some people are, by their design, more fragile and can't recover from a crash the way that you can. The type of devastating situations you have been in would have derailed their lives, maybe even indefinitely. But you, Madeleine, you are perfectly designed to crash."

I was both fascinated and frustrated by what she had to say. And I sat in a stunned sort of silence for a second or two. I was imagining myself as a crash-test-dummy buckled into the seat of a test car, hitting the wall at immense speed while my hinged limbs flailed about me wildly, unable to be ripped apart or broken. I watched that little scene play out in my mind before I blurted out, "But I don't want to crash. I'm tired of crashing. It's so painful and hard. I really don't want to do that again. I want to avoid crashing at all costs."

"Do you know what causes people the most injury in a crash or in a fall?"

"No. Not really,"

"Bracing for it. When you brace for a crash, you get stiff and rigid and your muscles tense. That tension, that stiffness is what causes your bones to break far more than they would if you were flexible and could roll with it. When you brace for a crash, it injures you more.

"Stop bracing for the crash."

We were both silent for a moment. And then she continued.

"You have done a lot of beautiful work, excellent work. You are in a good place. A safe place. A secure place. You cannot bubble wrap yourself so that life doesn't cause you any more pain. You, personally, are designed to learn from the hard things and to make your learnings useful to others so that maybe they don't have to crash like you did.

"Just because you are designed to crash doesn't mean you are predestined to continue crashing.

"Rest assured, no matter how hard you may crash again, if you do crash again at all, you will again rise up from a crash like a phoenix from the ashes. You don't have to bubble wrap yourself. You don't have to brace.

"You are ok and you will continue to be ok."

Her words washed over me like a calming balm. They massaged the aching parts of my heart and soothed them.

From that day forward, I have not worried about crashing.

Crashing, having Lightning Rod Moments, having hard circumstances, devastating losses, truly painful parts in the narrative of our life doesn't make our life bad. It doesn't make us bad, or wrong, or less.

It strengthens us.

Deepens us.

Softens us.

If we let it.

This sort of pain is not a punishment, it is a purification.

And when we can exit the pain, and recover from the hardship and gain some perspective, much awaits us. The gift is there—just beyond the horizon of the courage to look for it.

When we can find the courage to seek out the gift in these horribly hard, painful, dark places, we grow in a way that nothing else facilitates. That growth creates within us more capacity for love, a deeper well for peace, a new level of wisdom.

And that is why I choose to share with you some of the darkest, hardest, most difficult and devastating moments of my life—because I know that you have had them too. Different in circumstances and in context and in content, but similar in the heartbreak and in the pain.

Nobody wants to have to endure the hard parts.

Nobody is running into a crash, with joyful expectation.

Knowing that a crash is coming causes anguish. Knowing that it has happened does the same.

It is not easy.

Life is not an endless path of flowering, fragrant, gorgeous roses. All flowers, no thorns.

But there are flowers all around us.

And there are roses in our path.

It is our job to find them, to stop, to admire them, to delight in them and to bend down and breathe in their delicious fragrance.

Breathe deeply.

And let their beauty fill you up.

POST SCRIPTUM

I put the final touches on my manuscript many months ago and when my publisher asked me to write an Epilogue, I didn't know what else to say.

In the months since finishing the last chapter and tidying up the Exercises and going through the editing process over and over again, I worked with a partner to build a new business to help anyone who felt inspired by these pages to take the work deeper and go further with it. Legacy Leadership Institute is the crowning jewel of my work to date and I wanted to weave it into this book in a way that didn't feel salesy or dripping with self-interest. I thought about sharing the story of how this business came into being, of showing you how an entire business could be built so fast, or of giving you lots of incentives to check it out.

None of that felt correct.

The words just wouldn't flow. The story felt too current, too in-the-moment to be shared as a narrative.

Sam Horn, one of my invaluable book coaches, encouraged me to end this book with a story, and so I did, but Legacy Leadership Institute didn't find its way into those pages and the book felt incomplete without it.

There was one other thing that I had wrestled with including in the book that hadn't found a home either, so I decided to do something totally untraditional and add a Post Scriptum—a P.S.—to my book.

The book critics might not like it, and it might not be the way that things are done, but you know me by now and you know that when there isn't space for me, I make some.

So, now you know about Legacy Leadership Institute. If you're curious about it check it out at www.legacyleadershipinstitute.com. I would be delighted to see you inside of our community.

As for that other thing, it's a prayer.

I've not been shy about sharing that I'm a Catholic nor about my deep love of God. God is truly my beloved and whether I stay single or find a partner to share my life, God will always remain my beloved. His love has carried me through some of the hardest moments of my life.

When I set out to write this book, I did not want to devolve into self-pity, and I didn't want to be selfish or self-aggrandizing. I didn't want to share stories as a form of catharsis for myself. I wanted to share stories for you. To help you. To inspire you. To help you know that you are not alone in your struggles, that you are not alone in those quiet places of your heart that have worry and insecurity and pain.

We all struggle sometimes.

We all suffer from not being seen, not being heard, not feeling good enough or from some other hidden wound.

And I wanted you to know that there is hope.

There is hope of healing and of peace beyond the pain.

So, to keep that intention ever before me, I wrote a prayer that I would read every time I would sit down to write.

And I thought that the most fitting end to a book so full of realness, so full of the raw places, so fully exposing of who I am, where I have come from and how I have gotten to where I am now, would be to share this part of me too.

I have been afraid to alienate those of you who don't believe in God, to scare off those of you who might not pray, to insult those of you who don't believe in Jesus, but I don't walk in fear, and, if you've come with me this far, I trust in your strength and openness, and in the immense power of love.

So I'm sharing even this, my Luceat (Latin for "let it shine") Prayer Before Writing.

Luceat Prayer before Writing

Jesus, my Love, my Lord,
sweet Guardian of my soul, beloved Lover,
I dedicate this work to you and to the good
You want to do in this world.

I am unworthy, small, uninspired, sinful, fallen, dim.

You alone are the LIGHT of the World.
Permit that my words serve as light and salt
to increase your visibility,
to enrich and enliven the taste—the true authentic flavor—
of those who read these words.
May their minds be uplifted to you,
may their hearts be warmed to your love,
may they see themselves with the loving compassion,
the unwavering belief, the unshakable truth of your pure light.

Let me not stand in the way, blocking You,
but, in your loving mercy, guide me
to be an entryway, a portal, to You and You alone.

Let me express in words and story,
in vulnerability and strength,

*How, by journeying inwards, they can come
to a deeper understanding of who they are—
beloved sons and daughters of the most high God.*

*Let the princes and princesses in the house of the Father
come to know themselves more fully and
to discover or deepen their love
and knowledge of You.*

Let your image in them shine through my work.

*Let me be your docile paintbrush, in the company of St Thérèse.
Let me echo the words of St. John of the Cross.*

*Permit me, my Love, my Lord,
my most compassionate and sweet Jesus,
to stand on the shoulders of these giants.
Grant that, supported by their work, inspired by their lives
and resonating with their love of You,
grant that I too might shine the light of your love
on a world so desperately in need of You.*

With a heart bursting with love,

Madeleine MacRae.

ABOUT THE AUTHOR

ACCOMPLISHED SENIOR EXECUTIVE, ENTREPRENEUR, BEST SELLING AUTHOR, TOP TIER LIFE AND BUSINESS STRATEGIST

Madeleine Macrae serves as CEO and Founder for both Legacy Leadership Institute and Homepro Toolbox.

Madeleine is an accomplished corporate executive and a 4x founder with more than 17 years of experience leading, guiding, and growing businesses of all sizes. She understands how to harness the power of people and to catalyze growth.

Madeleine has empowered individuals and organizations across the globe with her live speaking, transformational coaching, and educational content. She artfully explores foundational principles to develop mastery in leadership, success, personal growth, and communication.

Her down-to-earth style makes even the most intimidating topics feel well within reach and her ability to blend cutting-edge information with fiery inspiration drives audiences—both live and virtually—to stand up and take action towards their growth and business objectives without losing sight of who they truly are and what they desire the most.

Made in the USA
Las Vegas, NV
16 February 2024